CW00794381

Desperate to be Loved

Little notes of self-discovery

Kelly Saward

Copyright © 2024 Kelly Saward

All rights reserved.

The right of Kelly Saward to be identified as the author of this work has been asserted by her in accordance with the Copyright, Designs and Patents Act 1988.

No part of this publication may be reproduced, stored in a retrieval system or transmitted in any form or by any means including photocopying, electronic, recording or otherwise, without the prior written permission of the rights holder, application for which must be made through the publisher.

ISBN 978-1-7384565-0-5 (hardback)
ISBN 978-1-7384565-1-2 (paperback)
ISBN 978-1-7384565-2-9 (ebook)

DESPERATE

a Mindful Journey

TO

from Anxiety and Fear

BE

to Love and Acceptance

LOVED

Kelly Saward

Meraki

(may-rah-kee) Greek

N: To do something with soul, creativity or love;
to put something of yourself into your work.

To Olivia and Summer,

The greatest love and learning come from you.
With this, I try and return a little bit of it back to you,
to keep with you forever.

Wherever you go, there I am!

Contents

To the person who inspired me when things looked dark.

To the person who helped me find the light inside.

To the person who showed me that oversharing
was quite simply being open with how I felt.

To the person who saw me for me.

The connection we all seek, the connection then felt …
there is nothing more than this.

The journey to who she was, to who she's always been.

Kelly Saward

Author's Note

FROM VERY YOUNG I loved writing stories, never sharing them, yet aware of the enjoyment in exploring where they'd go. The dream of being an author! Writing has always been something I come back to. It's like having a penfriend, that friend the little lost me deep down inside. It has been fun getting to know her again after all this time. I write in the dark times, on the difficult days and through the heartbreak. I jot down memories, funny moments, ask questions then explore them. Endless notes written and journals filled. Now I share a few of these little notes of self-discovery with you.

I realise that for me it really helped to not feel alone in how I was feeling, what I was experiencing. It helped to speak up and talk about it. It was invaluable to be heard – and not only that, listen to others, too. Through this I felt connected and ever so slowly things began to unravel. If you are wanting to explore meditation, I share my experience and struggle with it here in this book and just how helpful it has been, how it has given me the space to love my story. Despite the initial resistance, I now couldn't be without it. I even create my own meditations, and I have included a couple of those in this book. If you prefer guided meditations, you'll find a link to my recordings at the back of the book.

I share some of my own poems in here too, alongside tips, advice and little parts of myself, my story, in the hope and encouragement it helps you to see and welcome all of yours, too.

Anxiety kidnapped me for a while there, but I managed to escape, despite never thinking this possible. I share how that came about for me: why anxiety came along and how I changed my relationship with it, loosening its shackles.

This book isn't how to fix all your struggles, or how to find the love of your life, nor a quick resolution … I'm really selling it aren't I! Bet you're pleased you bought this one. This book is more of a friend: your support for whenever you've felt any of these things and to know you are not alone.

When telling my daughter I was publishing this book, she said, 'Are you, Mum? Really?' 'Yes,' I said, '"You have to believe to achieve!"' We had a little giggle as I love quotes. I use them all the time in the house and love that my children sarcastically quote them back at me. I explore them all the time too, as you will see throughout the book. She gave me a hug and said, 'Mum, you're a primary source.' Again, this really made me laugh and, loving to explore and question everything, I wrote it down and thought, *I love that! I am, aren't I?* We all are. We all have our own story, our first-hand experience in our life. In academic research, a primary source is defined as a document, a first-hand account or other source that constitutes direct evidence of an object of study. Well, I suppose that is what this is really. My first-hand account of my experience of what I have been through and my own evidence of that change: my personal study of self-discovery, pain and heartache. So, there we have it! The most useful things I have discovered I share here with you to simply explore and try if you want to.

If you're having a bad day, feeling disconnected or worried I want to help you feel not so alone with it, if I can. I hope through my words and my voice (if you choose to listen to any of the audio parts) that in some way you feel supported and loved, and have courage to explore whatever is present for you a little deeper.

If you already have a meditation practice, you may enjoy trying some of the ones I've shared in here. If you or someone you know experiences feelings of anxiety there are a few really helpful tips I found lifesaving in fearful moments. They are in the 'Mindful Moments' section at the back of the book.

If you've ever felt lost, lonely or unloved, desperate to feel that love too, you're not alone. You're never alone. I'm here with you as you read. It's going to be ok, even when it feels awful. I had to hit rock bottom to break through and I'm here: it is ok.

In discovering what helped me, I hope something helps you too. There's no right or wrong way to read it, you don't have to go cover to cover. You can just lean into what you need, just take it one page at a time.

One last note from me to you … When I read this back, when I write, if I feel I need to move the emotion through or connect deeper to what I'm feeling, I use a playlist. I'd have a soundtrack to the book if I could but that wouldn't suit everyone and it needs to be your own experience. So if it feels right, put some music on. I find the music holds me, enhancing my experience when I connect with what I write … what I question. My advice: pick up this book when you want, close your eyes, feel into your mood, your emotions and play songs that you feel connect you with that moment. Really feel it, own what you're feeling. Once more, lean in. Take what you need from what you read, it will never be the same for us all and that's what makes it beautiful. Pick it up, put it down, keep it, share it. Let me know what you think.

Lastly, a little fun fact for you about me: I love the moon. I love learning about it, working with it and bringing it into the way I write, the meditations I write and the meditation circles I run. (Ultimately, the moon doesn't feature in here at all as I have so much to learn, but if you want to find out more, I've listed one of my favourite books about the moon in the recommended reading.) I am a Cancerian; the moon is my ruling planet. Not only that, but I was also born under a full moon, on Friday the thirteenth! For anyone into this, I know! A divine feminine right here! There are 13 moon cycles, 13 is my lucky number and that's why the book is divided into 13 sections, led by 13 poems, with a few added extras in between.

Enjoy it all!

Love always, whole heartedly,

Kelly xxx

The words dropped into my soul, feeling them so deeply.

'Where exactly was it that I lost who I truly was?
When did I start to disappear?'

Desperate to be Loved

Standing before you, that look in my eyes,
Love and intense passion take me by surprise.
My body electric, my heart on fire,
I feel the burning, intense desire.

The rush it fills me, I'm locked in,
I have that knowing deep within.
Scared and excited all at once,
Fearful that my heart gets crushed.

I'm brave and open up once more,
Bare my soul, my heart, my core.
Body shaking, heart beats fast,
I really want this love to last.

Vulnerable, I give my all,
Yet still I stand and wait to fall.
Doubt takes over, lack appears,
Then come forward all my fears.

Not good enough, I'm far too much,
Second best and all that stuff.
Why can't someone put me first?
Rejection, oh! it is the worst.

I keep on searching for this love I long,
Wishing, hoping, holding on.
The patterns they repeat themselves,
What's wrong with me? Do I need help?

Gradually, I start to see,
The girl in the mirror looking back at me,
I haven't loved her in that way,
My love for her it went astray.

I began to show her love and compassion,
Then the magic started to happen.
The love I sought from everyone else,
I began to find it in myself.

Gently and slowly, I started to shine,
I now felt the love, the love that was mine.
It sat inside me all along,
My heart now beating full and strong.

Letting go is hard to do,
But you must have respect for you.
From this place I no longer ask why.
What's meant for me won't pass me by.

***

Chapter 1

Desperate to be Loved

FOR AS LONG as I can remember I've idealised love, right back to fairy tales, Disney movies ... dreaming of being loved in such a way. That pivotal movie moment when the girl gets swept off her feet. The deep look of love, the magical kiss. The happy ever after. That moment in *Dirty Dancing*: nobody wants to be left in the corner; instead pulled in close, adored, loved!

I love love. I love loving and I've always longed to be adored and seen for just who I am, swept of my feet.

When I think of this longing, I'm reminded of one of my favourite scenes in the well-known film *Notting Hill*. Countless times, I, too, have stood gazing up at a boy, my eyes telling their own story, asking for love, just like Anna Scott (played by Julia Roberts). Yet so often misunderstood, seemingly unheard.

Isn't this what we all want, to be loved? Looking deep into the eyes stood before you, wanting that same feeling back:

mirrored love. I know for me this has always been the way I lead, heart leaps forward, feet follow. The thing is, in being so desperate to be loved, I allowed my vision of love to blur my self-worth, meaning I so often received the wrong kind. Never first choice, not fully heard or understood but so desperate for love all the same, I lost myself instead.

Life happens and over time we encounter so much that this takes us on an unknown path. For some the fairy tale may come easy, for others not so much. It's difficult to meet the one who understands your version of love in the exact way you like to feel it. We all have the ability to love but our individual interpretation of it won't look the same (and nor should it), but understanding this can be hard, especially if throughout life you've been hurt, judged, been second choice, third choice or not even noticed. These things cut deep, and over time inform your own and others' impression of you. All the while we pour affection and time into trying to fit in and be oh so loveable.

To clarify, the desperation for this love rises in a constant search to be that perfect image seen in somebody else's eyes. A parent, a lover, a partner, a friend. Yet you slip away in trying to fit in. The journey ongoing.

But let me tell you something. This perfect love we look for: it's inside, it's you. You are the love you look for. I know, it doesn't feel like this at all, you want that deep connection, to be seen, heard and felt; understood fully just as you are, right? But to get somebody else to see you this way, you must see you, you must love you. When you do, the magic happens all by itself. You have the confidence to say no, to clearly see what's not right. You have the confidence to be just as you are and know that this is enough. You are enough! But getting to this point isn't always this easy. Believe me, I know! That's why I share some of my journey to love with you.

What is love?

IT IS DIFFERENT to every single one of us, but we are all so desperate to feel it. This begins the day we enter this world, feeling affection from our parents, our families. Making friends, evolving as we go and learning lessons.

For me, I love the depth of love, the warmth in the centre of my heart, belonging. The connection felt in the moment, the understanding when someone just gets you, they see you. There's nothing more than this. But life once more happens and things change, people change and again the loss is felt. You can be so deeply in love, yet it doesn't work out. Leading with my heart means I've had some very difficult lessons, some harder to understand than others. I'm grateful now, but I wasn't mid-heartbreak!

During my life I've always had a huge pull to music, loving to sing but not comfortable sharing my voice. Relating with the words of the song, finding deep meaning and connection. Lyrics and quotes help me uncover the answer to my all-important question: why? Why am I hurting so much? Why did that affect me? Why was I rejected? Why me! We've all been there. It's easy to constantly question ourselves, point the finger and blame, but again, this magic I speak of comes in the understanding you can unravel through outlets like journaling: the answers and realisations present themselves on the page, in the spaces given to ourselves when we simply listen to what we have to say.

I'm not perfect by any stretch but when I love I give my all, pouring love in and for some this being too much. I adapted myself to fit into the ideal, trying to be all I could for approval yet all the while I lost myself. Despite trying my best, I didn't fit and with this I let myself be walked over, criticised and accepted second place on more than one occasion. I didn't realise for a long time, but I was constantly striving to be someone I'm not, just to be accepted. The other harsh truth was that I didn't put myself first, ever. I didn't see my own worth and value and therefore never expected anything more than this. I was grateful to even come second place in somebody's eyes.

This pattern repeated itself in relationships, friendships, with family members, in employment. I was desperate to be loved and accepted so I just fell into more situations of the same. The more I perceived myself worthy of accepting second place, the more I attracted this. The pattern continued as long as I never felt enough.

For as long as I can remember I felt something was missing, being led the long way round for answers to this lack; parties, drinking, smoking and many detours on this search for something more. New jobs, a new car, a new house, a higher salary, holidays … the list goes on yet still the search continued. It wasn't until these past few months the penny dropped and I saw that what I had been striving for was love.

***

My anxiety had been creeping in for years until eventually the time came where I crashed, it was exhausting not being … me!

'Where exactly was it that I lost who I truly was?'

The words just dropped into my heart, this time feeling them so deeply. Tears began to fall and for some days they didn't stop.

It took me a while to unravel the route of it all, but I knew in this moment of turmoil that I couldn't walk in someone else's shoes any more. I was tired, drained, burnt out from trying to be someone that I'm not. The thing was, I was so fearful of walking in my own shoes. What did that look like? Who am I?

Buried beneath that never-ending search for love and belonging it became apparent I needed to see where I'd lost 'me' in the first place. This one moment, this question that spilled out of me, was that first step on the journey to return to who I truly am.

Time stood still for a moment as the tears dropped onto the wooden tabletop. My tears darkening the grains in the wood. I felt a shift immediately. It's one thing for someone else not to really see you, but quite another to not even see yourself, hidden under layers of coping. I was now brave enough to face this, and this was the moment in time where things changed for me. The very moment where life became too much was the same moment things would begin to unfold.

Throughout my lifetime the unknown would strike, and life continued to unravel. The only way I knew how to move forward was to put layers around myself. Layers of protection, or so I thought. These hefty layers took hold in many forms: anxiety, disconnection, unhealthy relationships, escape.

The layers had become so burdensome, I was bubble wrapped so tightly that I couldn't even see the centre any more, my heart heavy beneath it all. With each tear that fell, I felt a softening, a gradual opening back to me, back to love. Bubbles popping and finally releasing that pressure. IT'S OK TO FEEL! I could glimpse the light and with each breath it got brighter. I knew it wasn't going to be easy but the only way to find freedom, to find me, was to lean into how I felt.

Spending time in nature released something creative in me: poems began to form part of the healing process of my journey. Song after song played on repeat until I found my own personal lesson within the lyrics. Quotes explored to find connection back to myself. And this was key for me: a safe space to listen, to feel, to connect, to write and explore just what was happening in my own time. I was now giving myself this gift, the gift of time.

My journaling continued, many pages written and burnt. We intuitively know what we need, even if we can't give it a name. Writing has always helped me pull through, providing a place to reveal my voice. Back then it was simply a way to express myself. I now call this journaling; you may choose to call it something else.

A time will come when passion conquers fear, the fire burning so strong that everything else is silenced. The secret is to jump on it, dig deep and believe so it doesn't once more pass you by. That's where I am today: for over four years I accumulated a pile of papers, my story, my guide – and this time I haven't burnt the pages, I share them here with you. Wrapped up in these pages I share the help I discovered during my journey back home to myself.

***

FOR SO LONG I always needed a plan, a routine, constantly living in busyness, planning holidays and outings to validate I'd done enough and had control over what's coming. In turn I was completely avoiding what I truly needed.

In 2019, six months before the Covid-19 lockdowns, I had a mini breakdown (or breakthrough, as I now call it). I went on a girly holiday with two of my friends who were unable to come to my wedding in Antigua (which I then never made it to, thanks to the pandemic). We'd been looking forward to it for ages; whenever we got together, we had the best time. We were originally due to be flying to Gran Canaria, but that didn't happen. Thomas Cook collapsed the week before we were due to fly, and we had to change our holiday. We were optimists, it didn't matter. Benidorm was the only reasonable option for our travel dates and so off we went! We had great weather and such a giggle as always, but I knew I didn't feel quite myself.

I felt I didn't deserve to go, I shouldn't. I felt guilty leaving the children and spent days and weeks leading up to the break away organising dance runs, school runs, shopping, lists upon lists, upon lists! I had lists for the lists! Laying out clothes for their days to come.

I burnt out at work, working with no lunch break day after day, cramming in as much work as I could into my days with not a moment to spare. As soon as I left the office, off to collect the kids and mum role would kick in, through till bedtime I would fill every moment with something to take myself away from my fearful thoughts. I never made any time for myself and I would flop in a heap with exhaustion at the end of the day, before it began again.

Looking back on it now, I see that I'd allowed it all to happen, but I had to learn from the struggle. I didn't want a break; I didn't want to stop and have time to be with my thoughts. I had waited on my family because I'd chosen to do so. I'd exhausted myself for far too long as I thought that's what I should do. There was a lot of tension at work between me and my partner as it was a family-run business – a story I won't venture into – but it weighed heavily, took its toll and things couldn't go on as they were. My passion and soul had been suppressed but I knew there was a deep inner strength, something bigger than the fear to help me release it all again, but I pushed it down, feeling like it was easier to maintain my anxious habits rather than face change. Like anything, I assumed the fault lay with me. Even as I write this, the old voice of judgement arises once more: *I should be spending time with the children … I haven't got time to take a break … There is no time! … Am I selfish for prioritising me? … I feel I'm letting others down.*

I was permanently trying to do and control EVERYTHING: every little detail at work, at home, preplanning. I tell you, this is a draining, tiring place to be. Control is a common coping mechanism when suffering and that was certainly the case for me. My lack of sleep was also beginning to be a real problem (despite feeling constantly exhausted, I just couldn't switch off).

Once I'd tried to plan and control each aspect of anything I could get my hands on I was packed and ready to go. My friends arrived and we jumped in my car and off we went. Of course, I'd booked the holiday, the airport parking, I was driving. Again, any one of us could have done this and they'd have been happy to do so, but I had to manage everything.

We got to the airport and had a great time: breakfast, drinks, waiting for the flight and we were off. Freedom! We landed, straight to the hotel – perfect. I had everything I needed: sun, all-inclusive, endless drinks, my best friends and a break! I knew my girls were fine at home with my loving partner – I could relax.

The thing is, I couldn't. I just couldn't do it. Don't get me wrong I was having a wonderful time, we had an amazing break. It was filled with laughter, dancing and friendship, memories I'll always cherish but I still couldn't sleep. I began to feel pains in my chest and as each day passed, I was more and more tired, my anxiety at its most severe in the dark of night.

For years I'd wanted a break but when I finally got my break, the years of control beforehand meant I couldn't switch off, I wasn't able to relax. I couldn't even read a book or have a proper sun-soaked doze by the pool. My friends snoozing beside me. I remember one day at the side of the pool my friend pulled out her book. It was a book on being positive. She asked my other friend and I to sit up and close our eyes, which we did, sitting on the edge of the sunbed. She asked us out of ten how we felt. I think I said eight, my other friend I think the same. She read the positive feel-good page and asked us again what we now felt. I had gone down to a seven, my friend up to a nine. I will never forget my friend's face (I can now laugh at the moment we shared that day). She was shocked, exclaiming, 'What! That's not right. This is meant to make you feel better!' I got two things from this: I was not in a good headspace so anything could have been read out and my undertone would always create this slightly dampened negative response. I also realised we aren't always in the same place. The younger me – despite feeling a bit shit – would probably have gone with the higher number to people-please but I had at least grown enough by this point to say how I truly felt. I knew when I sat with my thoughts I'd feel scared, anxious. Fearful, hence the endless distractions in my day.

The entire time I was away in Spain, any time I wasn't expressing how I felt or if I wasn't distracted by something, there was a background hum of worry. A feeling in my chest I just couldn't shake. Am I having a heart attack? Anxious thoughts filled in mind. Every single night I had no more than three hours' sleep. Ok not going to lie, we were reliving our late teens, out every night on the strip till 5am, dancing, laughing, letting the good times roll. However, despite the late nights I couldn't sleep past 8am at best and with each day that passed the background pains in my chest and constant unease became slightly more prominent.

The day we flew home came and our flight was late in the evening, 11.30ish. We had a great last day; I almost didn't want it to end but of course I wanted to see the family. We boarded the flight, landed around 1.30am and headed to the car. Driving home I felt tired but knew it was late. After the drive and dropping my friends home, I drove the last part of the journey not feeling too great and pulled in the drive with joy, happy to be home. I crept up the stairs after the most wonderful welcome from my dogs and got into bed. My partner happy to see me home but despite the incredible tiredness I couldn't sleep again. This was when I finally snapped.

I'd reached the comfort of my home and it all hit me – burnout. Breakdown, and the worst panic attack I'd ever had.

***

The morning I'd arrived home and crawled into bed I knew it was only a matter of hours before the children were up. I couldn't sleep at all. By the time they came in, their lovely little faces so excited to see me, ready for Mum to take them to school as I always did, I couldn't do it; I didn't know what was happening. I put on a brave face, got up with them and did what I could, my partner shielding me from having to show how sad I was, how scared I was. (On reflection I don't think he understood either, how could he?

I'd just been away, he expected me to be rested. I expected me to be rested, that's what it says on the tin, right? Yet I couldn't have felt further from it.) I couldn't take the girls to school; I couldn't leave the house. We chatted, I kept a brave face on and off they went to school with Dad. I stayed at home, terrified of what was happening. In some crazy thought I had initially told work I'd be in that day after a few hours' sleep, but I cancelled that and didn't make it in for the whole week – again so unlike me. I sat at home, crying, feeling lost, burnt out and completely done in from the non-stop, self-inflicted running around I'd been doing for years. The suppression of so much emotion.

During this week at home, unable to leave the house I had a panic attack – luckily, the kids were asleep. I thought I'd had one before but believe me I hadn't. If you've had one before, you yourself know, the feeling is like no other: nothing but intense fear. I called 111, having convinced both myself and my partner I may be having a heart attack, and the paramedics arrived. Plugged into an ECG in the middle of the night I could see the sadness in my partner's eyes, he looked helpless as he tried to reassure me a million times I was fine, but the irrational thoughts and panic took over within me. The paramedics confirmed it was indeed anxiety, gave me some advice and off they went. Over the coming days I had a lot of support at home and each day got a little bit easier. The following week I returned to work and started to roll back into my routine.

At the time I was also planning my wedding for April 2020, which as you know wasn't to be: the first lockdown cancelling so many plans. As I write this, we are in the third lockdown. Who'd have thought it. Still no new date for the wedding, but that's ok. As I keep being reminded, things happen when they're meant to.

I knew I still wasn't myself, I felt something had shifted. I've always had my own opinion and would go against the grain if required. This trait led to people thinking I was rude, sometimes selfish but I was also complimented on being organised and in control. Everyone has different views and that's ok. With my drive still somewhere within I knew for my daughters, my family and most importantly myself I had to sort this out. One of my friends at work could see I was struggling and not my usual self and recommended a reflexologist to me. Our first session was a real eye-opener: she pointed something out to me that hadn't really registered previously and once this had hit home, I opened up and could feel movement within.

I got an awful lot out of my reflexologist; she was more than this and when I heard she was moving away just before lockdown I wasn't quite sure what to do. I started practising mindfulness and meditation, which I had tried before actually – a fair few times in fact throughout my life but never sustained it for longer than a few scattered months of meditating, always thinking I was doing it wrong. I saw another reflexologist who worked with colour and cards, and I loved this too.

Whilst this was hard to suffer, it was an incredibly special turning point in my life. This breakthrough started my journey back to find 'me'. Knowing I was always there. Always her – I was just lost in there.

I didn't see it, or believe in me!

***

DURING LOCKDOWN, ALTHOUGH I needed to work from home for the family business, the progress I'd already made over the previous few months meant I knew I needed something for me. I was drawn to meditating each day, having meditated on and off for years yet never embodying it. I was enjoying this new habit sticking, and soon mindfulness also became present in more of my day. During the pandemic, I realised how fortunate I am in many ways, surrounded by love. I found me – my dharma. I even miss the lockdown period at times: the time I'd been gifted to spend on me. I now ensure I have a little time for me each day and practise the things I have learnt which healed me.

I attended a course to become a mindfulness and meditation teacher and I can honestly say it changed my life. My focus changed. My view changed. It solidified what I needed to do. I've always been passionate about mental health and healing, and this feels like my way to give back and help others. I educated myself on lots of different things through audiobooks, journaling and meditation. Learning from others, too. The people I have met in the past four years are like no other and gradually my practice and teaching have developed their own style.

A year on from my breakthrough in 2019, in October 2020 I started an Instagram page for my mindfulness practice: @room_478.

Sharing my thoughts on social media re-ignited my love of writing, I would write things that inspired me that I'm passionate about. I would post quotes and start thinking about what they meant to me, so I kept writing and writing. As mentioned, unknowingly for much of my life I had been healing through song and quotes, I continue to unravel my story in this way, I feel the pain, find connection, and heal a little part of what has once hurt.

But I was always hiding behind the busyness, listening to that negative voice worrying about what others thought. I would have never thought of publishing this book if I was still filled with other people's judgements of me. What they think – that's on them, not me. As said by the Dalai Lama, 'Listening to someone else's judgement is saying you have more confidence in their opinion of you than your own!' A line I've read again and again … Why do we do this?

If you feel like I did back then: lost, exhausted, sick of the endless pretending to be someone you're not, I hope the words, thoughts and poems I share with you can inspire you to uncover your true self. I have realised that I've always been in here, I just got a little lost for a while. I hope just one part of this helps you too.

New Doors

Flowing through my fingers, the thoughts they
leave my mind,
Present in this moment, anxiety left behind.
I feel a little scared but excited all the same,
The pen it gives me freedom and acceptance of
the shame.

Writing is the key to the centre of my heart,
Opening that knowing when I don't know where
to start.
Loss and pain are felt in every single bone,
But without it, I'd have never braved the
wondrous unknown.

The gratitude I feel brings a smile across my face,
This now shines throughout my soul, anxiety
replaced.
Dare to see the future, let go to it all,
Live out your adventure, listen to your call.

***

Chapter 2

New Doors

SO MANY DOORS are ahead waiting for you to just open them.

Leaving behind our thoughts can be difficult, but when you write down how you feel, fully emerging in those feelings, however painful, something magical happens. When I give those thoughts space to be seen and noticed, as I write them down they leave my mind. Seeing them laid out in front of me rather than becoming them, now instead I get to see them. An understanding starts to unravel in front of my eyes. What once felt overwhelming now feels manageable. For a second, whilst present in this moment, anxiety is relinquished.

Anxiety has been my go-to coping mechanism for so long that at times I almost feel anxious to not be anxious! As mad as it sounds, the unravelling of this hidden addiction still sometimes catches me out. How the mind works in such a way, that habits become fully stuck in motion. So many times, without even realising it, when anything became too much, I would obsess about a new health issue. Anxiety taking a tight grip on my thoughts. My focus then on the loop of fear rather than on the sadness felt deep inside. I must catch myself even now. I see that the more I delve deeper into understanding my journey, there's more space available for emotion to rise from deep inside. So again, I am entrenched in the battle of anxiety versus healing. Writing is the key to the centre of my heart. Each time I reach for a pen I create an opening, knowing I rarely know where to start. And so I begin; I explore what's present with little attachment to what ends up on the page but instead notice a movement within. Another door opens.

***

To FIND MAGIC around you, you must carry magic inside you. This can be hard to do with so much social pressure and information taking us away from the simple joys in each day. But it is there, and it's found in all the little things you sometimes can't see or touch.

Harry Potter has been a much-loved, overplayed, yet always welcomed feature in my house. The mystery, the magic, the belief in something beyond what we see in front of us. Both of my girls have always loved magic and throughout life held a belief in something they couldn't see or touch. In turn, growing up I see that they believe in themselves, in others and understand there is more to life than you can see. It's beautiful.

Those who do not believe in magic will never find it, never find that wonder, feel that excitement. I'm not saying go out and buy a magic wand but simply take time to sit in stillness and see what can be found.

There is magic all around us, within us. New doors available for you to open, you just need to unlock them. Our very existence is magical. To live a life without feeling magic is a life with no belief. I am reminded of this very magic when I now don't hear those magic footsteps run down the stairs on Christmas morning. There are mixed views on Father Christmas but to me, believing in something that you can't see is important. When my own children arrived at that pivotal moment, I wanted to instil in them the very importance of believing in something you can see, to keep the magic alive. There is so much we can't see but we feel it, we have that inner knowing, the sense of magic, endless possibility. We've all felt it in some walk of life and that's what leads us to the new doors. Don't lose that.

***

It can be hard to access this place inside where nothing is impossible. Life happens to us, and this carries impact. Loss and pain are felt in every single bone, and it can seem like there is no way out at times. I have faced loss and pain in different forms throughout my life so far and each time I have dealt with such challenges in various ways, each utterly contrasting with how I deal with such events now; it's as though the lessons reappear when I'm stronger so as to heal that pattern. I've buried as much as I can, kept smiling and lost myself in a world of busyness and distraction. Binge drinking, smoking, late night parties. In later years when becoming a parent, the distractions merged into extreme busyness so as not to stop and feel anything. I was always somebody who said 'Well, I just haven't got time'. The truth was I didn't want time, I wanted to permanently be on the go so as not to sit with the deep issues buried inside. As said throughout this book, anxiety eventually became the biggest addiction of all and in turn it took me down. Wrapped up in a constant focus on my children's health, and my own, that I didn't have time to feel. My focus and time were spent just living in a state of fear and eventually I burnt out. Yet I have gratitude for even the struggles now, as without it I'd have never found the courage and conviction to tread a new path.

***

WE HAVE THE power to choose one thought over another, we just need to know how. Firstly, allow them to show up, to be present, just sit with them and then space will open up to see outside of this, to see the joy right in front of you, in simple things often missed. When we do, those new doors open and you won't even need to fumble for the key. As you read this, it may seem unthinkable; I have been there, but I promise you, we do have the power to choose. Those thoughts do not control us, and freedom is within reach.

The thoughts we give attention to, do indeed get bigger or multiply, or quite simply take over all headspace if we let them. This is why it's important we pick the right ones. We have the power to change our direction of focus. I do not know enough about the science to put it all in this book, but there are plenty of wonderful books with a deeper understanding of how the neurones wire together, causing neural pathways to take on the habits and suddenly off you go, lost in thought, so to speak. Yet the wrong ones. My aim in sharing my journey with you is to let you know how I came to see that just like choosing not to have the second packet of crisps in the pub, I can also choose not to have regular unhealthy thoughts.

We all feel stress at some point and for each of us different things will trigger our stress response. The problem is when we get sucked into stress becoming our natural response to situations, it turns into habit. This regular behaviour then shows up repeatedly.

Stress and anxiety can be associated with responses such as eating, drinking, smoking, going out, even excessive exercise and many more. Everything in moderation is a sign of embracing a healthy day-to-day lifestyle, but when the choice becomes an escape it's time to take a deeper look within. Subconsciously, you may bring on the stress to enjoy the responses and so forth. It can become a vicious cycle or pattern that in turn becomes almost routine. We may not even need to have a reason for feeling stressed but there we are again – stressed out! I'm sure every one of us has previously even enjoyed sharing at some point just how stressed we are. When you have validated your stress, the reward then becomes the trigger. Be it an extra night at the pub this week; a visit to the shop to buy that 'last' packet of cigarettes; a bar of chocolate justified as it's a crap day. You get the gist.

At work, it can almost become a default part of the day, a domino effect. One person is stressed, then the next, before the day is out the whole office is stressed. Numerous trips to the shop, planned pub visits for the evening. You may only hear the word 'work' and already the stress is there! Do we really want stress as part of our routine? I think the answer is no.

We can choose where to focus our attention and once we master this the stress will be less present. Of course, we will always experience stress at times, but we don't need to experience the constant levels of stress we put ourselves under. We don't need to become it. We shouldn't be finding gaps within a stressful day. Instead, the day may only have stressful moments which we can observe, and from which we can manage. Part of the problem with stress is that we are always thinking about what's to come. To cut the stress in half immediately we need to stop and focus just on what we can control in today, rather than take yourself off into past or future events that are not in our control.

The gratitude I feel brings a warm feeling when I think of how different life becomes when you find magic in things that were there all along. The moments lost in the fear and panic.

Meditation practice helps you become more mindful, which in turn enables you to find moments of magic. Paying mindful attention to something outside of your thoughts, even for a moment, is the first step to more choice, making those new doors accessible. This can be anything at all: your breathing, music, cooking, a walk. The act of focusing on something can divert your thoughts. To begin with, you may only be able to stay with it for a second before you are called back by your mind, but just know, that's ok! Let the thoughts come up and instead of trying to rush ahead and find resolution, give the thought a little space, write it out, simply observe it and it may surprise you but you can't hold on to one thought forever, so by giving it space it usually softens in its own time. Give yourself the choice to now be with something else, possibly notice new things, not only about your environment but also about you.

We all have a choice but regularly we tell ourselves we don't, or lead ourselves to believe that there isn't another option. Time being a big block for many. Money also another common one so as not to even explore a new adventure. Yet we have so much opportunity in today and this leads to even more choice, new doors, but we miss them in our habitual routines. Next time you think you haven't got time, pause for a second … surely there's a way to explore some part of whatever it is.

Picture this: a busy mum with two children, working part-time, pick-up from two different schools. Still needing to sort something for dinner and the dream of drafting a book. It all seems too much, no time, the task too big so the dream shuts down.

Now picture the same mum: same tasks, same dream. She wakes up and instead of rushing to everyone's needs, writes a paragraph of her thoughts, not a whole book but she takes a moment to connect with what she enjoys. She does the school run, goes to work and instead of jumping on the 'I'm stressed!' train, she takes herself out to the car for five minutes and writes another small paragraph. She doesn't stop at the shop on this occasion as something will do; five different dinners do not need to be cooked today and once this has been done, she writes down what she did for herself today. The result: a smile at the small win of making the choice to take a step to do something she enjoys.

We can all make different choices; we can all feel magic

inside. We just need to choose one thought over another, even if it's small, so you can feel that pause and connect with something for you. Take a step towards the door, even if you can't yet walk through it.

These small moments are the big moments, they now shine throughout my soul, displacing anxiety. I make choices to focus – even if just for a moment – on something I enjoy, to reconnect to myself. After all, I seemed to have hours to ponder over extreme events that never even happened!

***

WE ALL LOOK to the finish line at times, yet often feel so overwhelmed by mountainous tasks we put on ourselves that we end up choosing not to engage at all. To finish you must start, and by finish, I mean just accomplish something of meaning from what you set out to do. It isn't failure if you sign up to a course and don't complete it. Just give it a go. It may not be for you and that's ok. Focus on the fact that you're trying, you started, and your finish line will be where it will be. Remove all the pressure about finishing and you'll notice how new doors open all the time. The most important thing is to choose to give what feels right a go and then know it's ok to head to a new door, a different experience if that's what's calling you. As a nation we are rather good at beating ourselves up over what we *haven't* done and impart little praise for what we've given a shot. The finish isn't important, it's the endeavour.

Putting things off is something we all do. I tend to put off the big jobs, the ones I don't fully understand or the seemingly out of reach goals as self-doubt takes over, or again the 'no time', 'not enough money' saga strikes! Yet the culprit that holds me back most is when I worry about what others may think. Judgement! It's happened about a thousand times over the past four years whilst hanging on to this book! Imposter syndrome, a commonplace concept nowadays, as we are not alone remembering those moments of judgement! But it strikes all the same and I freak out. I feel I can't do it; I don't feel confident, good enough, clever enough and so on. It's such a shame that throughout life we take this on. Sadly, it's so common, we often sit in a place of thinking someone else is better, or I may get laughed at, or something else to this effect and these thoughts, the words of others, they sink in and damage our self-belief, our self-esteem. The point is they are just words, not our identity; we can choose to simply notice these words and not consume the damaging impact.

New doors open when we realise our worth. Taking the small moments to do those things you enjoy fuels this, your value. You see that you matter, what you want is also important. There is only one of you and you are amazing. You are capable of huge things. From here you begin to access the confidence to step out of your comfort zone – to get started on the bigger things. Just drafting this book proves this to myself. I have written millions of words in my lifetime and never wanted to share them, I chose to keep them to myself for fear of people judging my story. But now I see if I had read more stories like this, knowing I wasn't alone with how I felt, I would have found support in this.

I love writing and now I see that the real healing comes when sharing, especially when finding space to feel safe with others who can be open, too. This strengthens each time I hold space, leading a group in meditation: at the end I see the new doors opening not only for me but inside themselves, too. The conversation at the end is a beautiful moment. I find more and more that there are people who will listen, and most of the time all any of us want is someone to hear us: not fix or provide answers, but just listen.

Through journaling, the fear softened, the answers came, the doors opened and I went inside. We have the key inside ourselves, the answers are right there in the choices and small steps. Mindful awareness of what we choose and why leads us to inquiry; meditation is a great space to just be with what is. Even if that's a thought filled meditation, the growth comes in just witnessing what's present. I can see how far I've come. Making a choice to stop reminds me to take a small step towards whichever door I want to open, what to focus on each day; that is one foot in front of the other. One step at a time. Journaling may not currently seem natural to you, but I'd encourage exploring it a little: there is no rule to it, just write it out.

These doors are available to you too.

***

Journaling has helped me understand myself and listen to what I have to say.

The page listens when no one else does.

My head is often full of thoughts. I know it's natural for thoughts to come into our minds but when they get

34

overwhelming it can be hard to cope, to even focus on the day-to-day things.

Journaling helps our brains regulate emotions and turns our attention inwards to acknowledge our thoughts and feelings. It's such a healthy way to help with anxiety and has a huge number of benefits.

Some include:

- Reducing stress and anxiety.
- Improving our memory function.
- Sharpening our brain.
- Giving us a point of focus.
- Strengthening our emotional and immune functions.
- Lifting our mood.

There are no rules: you can write as little or as much as you want.

Do you listen to what your thoughts are trying to tell you? Try writing them down, it's so therapeutic. It is as though you've whispered these thoughts privately to yourself, your journal is just for you. Once you've written them down things start to become clearer. Carrying less weight, the thoughts now on paper, having less weight and power over you.

Journaling is my way of expressing gratitude, reminding myself of what I want, who I am. It hugely reduces my anxiety by clearing out my thoughts; I can rationalise them.

Journaling reminds me of all the things I've learnt, which

helps me continue to combat my anxiety every day. In turn I've summarised them in here (well, I hope so) in the hope they help somebody else.

Journaling is a way I kindly communicate with myself. But I must always remember to put the pen down and feel into what has risen. To be curious about what was ready to come to the surface, what is now present to be explored and bring compassion to this process.

I like to pause for a moment, meditate even for a short while and see what comes to me in the open space, then journal around this. I invite you to try this too.

***

DON'T PUT OFF something you want to do out of fear of others' opinions. Those judgements are a reflection on the person judging, not on you. You can start now, however small a step you take or how scary it seems. The more scared you are, the more passion inside there is to let out!

An important journal prompt when enquiring why you aren't doing what it is you want is to just simply sit with the question. What's holding you back?

Try to visualise what's behind the door you want to walk through. What's in your vortex and what exactly is it that is stopping you reaching for the key? There is no right or wrong answer here either, just choose to stop for a minute, write the question down and whatever comes to mind first just go with that.

Remember that the page won't judge you, so just freely write what comes up and from here you can see what's possibly in your way. By exploring this question, alone, you've taken a step towards making a different choice. A choice towards something you want to do.

Albert Einstein reminds us: 'Insanity is doing the same thing over and over again and expecting different results.'

We know change takes us out of our comfort zone. All the self-limiting beliefs rise once more. Fear of judgement, not good enough, too old, not old enough, not fit enough, not clever enough, not the right time. The list goes on. This time make the choice to reach into your subconscious, go past your ego. The only person holding you back is you; you can make a change and you can start today – even if the change is small. You want to open a bakery: make a bread roll!

Remarkable things start with small steps!

***

WHY WASTE MUCH time in a place of fear? Because you can't always help it, that's why. I know! It's important to remember that there is a place for fear, it's a natural response to threat and can be very handy, but when anxious habits and constant stress take over, we train our minds to think our bodies are under permanent threat even when it's not the case. Unfortunately, our imagination can focus on this too, the mind in overdrive. It's exhausting, time-consuming and scary!

All this worry takes you away from creation. The worry becomes a habit and I have to remind myself that fear and worry never create helpful habits.

My imagination has jumped on the worry train more times than I can count! Misuse of our imagination can bring angst and even prolonged physical pain, without anything ever actually happening. It is just our mind imagining these thoughts. The thoughts are not actual events, just our imaginations running off to worst-case scenarios.

With mindfulness I've learnt to stop my imagination working overtime, to be present and experience the enjoyment of so many wonderful things and surrender to NOW.

My imagination can now see great things: love, destinations I want to visit, dreams I want to accomplish. Worry no longer fills my mind. Of course it pops in, but it doesn't consume me any more. Mindfulness and meditation have enabled me to be where I am now.

Our imagination can take us to wonderful places, it is a great and powerful force. Spend a little time finding yourself, be playful. Ask yourself questions and see where the path leads you instead. Take control of your imagination today and steer it away from the fear, take it back to those fun-filled dreams.

If you know what it feels like to worry too much of the time, try and be a little more mindful each day. In time the worry will assume less of your imagination and free your mind.

***

You CAN DO it … 'Burst the bubbles that are not letting you be free'.

These bubbles could be anything to you …

- Old habits holding you back.
- Thinking things will never change.
- Waiting for the perfect time.
- Waiting to be in the right frame of mind.
- Worrying about money.
- Thinking you're not good enough.
- Negative voices in your head saying 'don't'.
- Assuming you know you'll fail.
- Other people's judgements.
- Negative people in your life.

When you start bursting these bubbles it creates space for the wonderful things to come into view and enables you to flourish.

Don't listen to that person telling you – *you can't* or *shouldn't*. How do they know?

When is the perfect time to do it?

Who cares if they judge you.

Don't keep doing everything to please everyone else, you matter too.

***

WE KNOW THAT we learn from our mistakes. We also know that if we take that jump, we may even reach further than we thought. Surely it's better to try than to never try at all.

If you have a strong feeling and know you should be doing something different you owe it to yourself to at least try it. What's the worst that can happen? It doesn't work out. That's ok, you've had a new experience and learnt from that. The best that can happen is that you get to be free – and be you! Not hidden behind others' opinions and self-judgements.

It's ok to free those thoughts, people or factors so that you can take a leap forward and be free to be all you are capable of.

Go on, burst some of your bubbles today.

Believe in you, make a choice to see yourself and feel the magic.

Dare to see the future, give in to it all; live out your adventure, listen to your call.

The door is right in front of you, you just need to open it.

Lost and Found

Sat aside the river, peace is all around,
Silence now feels golden, only nature sounds.
I no longer need distractions filling up my mind,
My body now it has the chance to feel and just
unwind.
The rain begins to fall, the droplets one by one,
I watch them hit the water and then comes out
the sun.
Change is always happening, moments passing by,
Yet sometimes we don't see it, I often wondered
why.
Distractions always present, time on my own
once feared,
Smiling through the sadness and holding back
the tears.
But now my mind is clearer, not always feeling
lost,
The keeping up it stole my time and at a huge
great cost.
My mental health did suffer, anxiety took hold,
Embarrassed to share my story and let it just
unfold.
Yet now within the silence, the moments, the
subtle pause,

I explore it all and find my strength and welcome
all my flaws.
By opening I find myself and much to my
surprise,
All that I was looking for, sat right here inside.

***

Chapter 3

Lost and Found

I DIDN'T REALISE quite how lost I had become, always searching, grasping at constant distractions to take me away from truly feeling how I felt. For as long as I can remember I liked being busy. I never liked spending time on my own and in the moments not filled the TV would go on. Any real issues which arose somehow got pushed down and I continued to plough through. Over time and unbeknown to myself I found anxiety as a cover. Any time something became a bit too much I would obsess about a pain, a feeling, a new sensation present and slip down the rabbit hole, turning to Google for advice. Big mistake.

I hadn't really been aware of how long this had gone on for, but after much soul-searching and finally taking the time to understand myself, I see that I had been looking for distractions for much of my life. Going out excessively, drinking, smoking, late nights, working longer hours, no breaks. The distance growing, the connection to self breaking down, hidden.

It's odd to think how much time we spend getting to know others, even celebrities we've never met. The ins and outs known of so many yet the person we spend our entire lives with, ourselves, often gets pushed aside, misunderstood and lost along the way. We often participate in negative self-talk. Not providing the same compassion to ourselves that we outwardly impart on others.

Words can cause pain and words can cause joy. Words express how and what we think and feel so to keep hearing criticism (whether it's from others or yourself), it chips away.

My life lessons to date have been a mix of both good and bad, I wouldn't change them. I've learnt in recent years that the difficult times show the strength I've gained. The lesson I needed to face would keep showing up until I realised I could now meet those challenges and then move through them with love – no longer lost, instead able to find a way through. I never liked the word 'fail' until my daughter pointed out that it simply stands for '**first attempt in learning**'. I like this positive spin and have carried it with me ever since. So, I see now, I have indeed failed but each time I've got back up and had another attempt to get it right. Well, what's right for me. After all, we are all walking our own paths and learning our own lessons. What for me may be a failure may be somebody else's win and vice versa. I've come through ok. Better than ok, in fact, and I see now that the way we see ourselves is the most important thing. Not getting lost viewing yourself through somebody else's eyes. As where is the use in this?

I'll never forget the time somebody said to me 'Isn't it strange that every single person you meet will see a different version of you?' Their view will contrast to yours and so too from everybody else you meet. The way your personality is viewed, your soul, even; each adding to this snapshot they hold of you. Which means no matter what others think or feel about you, it will always be different to how you see of yourself. Creating and connecting with this positive self-image is so important, embracing all of your journey.

I see now, after reframing what I've been through and where I've come from with gratitude, all the riches I needed were with me the whole time and when I started loving myself, they started to grow too. I had more time. More freedom. The answers inside, now in finding my own way, I find I take myself down a different rabbit hole to find the answers themselves; a whole new insight! An adventure!

***

Throughout 2020 and into 2021, I like to compare myself to a butterfly, starting in the cocoon. No doubt questions emerged for us all during this time. For me, I just kept asking. This time, however, the answers didn't come from Google. Nor was I any longer reliant on the news or social media. Instead, I gained a huge power in trusting myself whenever anything felt uncertain. I came back to this place again and again: journaling, questioning and moving forward in this way. I started to do what was good for me, what made me feel uplifted. Not always doing the 'right' thing either; the thing that made others happy, the people-pleasing version of self-destruction at times. For my own good I had to distance myself from people who relied too heavily on me or made me feel bad for not seeing them. As an Empath, I heavily take on and feel emotions from others. Having spent far too much time feeling bad about myself in the past, in order to heal I couldn't carry other people's emotions and had to start bringing awareness to myself.

In this period of standstill I also had the luxury (though I initially thought this was hell), of being able to be with how I felt and tune into what I needed in the present moment. This was extremely uncomfortable to start with and hard going to be honest. With my default distractions out of reach, I really had to work at this new way of being.

Of course, I was still available for friends in need, a chat if needed, showing love and support to those close to me, but I had to stop feeling in to and becoming emotionally involved with other people's lives. I was now learning how to say no and recognise my own needs. If I had read this very paragraph myself some years ago, I would have thought this a little heartless and selfish, but my point being, we've all been an unwitting accomplice in taking time away from ourselves when we really shouldn't. We also don't need to keep doing all the time! One of my favourite quotes when training to become a mindfulness teacher was to remember 'We are human beings – not human doings!' More than this: spiritual beings having a human experience! I love this sentiment and always come back to this in the present moment, reminding myself to simply 'be' every now and then instead of doing. Experience instead of control.

So, for a while I was going to embrace 'being' as best as I could. When I felt I couldn't be all the time I would just notice that and come back again and again. I could feel each time I came back to this place that I was doing what was right. I decided after long enough to confront the issues I was having head on, and as each one rose, I sat with it, however uncomfortable. Much of this time was spent writing it out; other times doing nothing at all. Crying, listening, understanding, not understanding, but each and every time I came back to just being with how I felt and not trying to change it. This wasn't easy: people I cared about got hurt in the process, I had to spend less time with certain people and not show up as I once had. But I see now the time comes when enough is enough and there is only so much any one of us can take. To follow your intuition, to stick by what truly matters, this is strength. Strength we all have inside of us but sometimes we don't feel capable, or worthy of what we know all along.

I see the strength is found in being vulnerable and seeing what's happening, what's right in front of you. Not necessarily to fix anything, more so just to acknowledge it and not push it away. The thing is the doubt kept creeping back in. Again, and again my old thought patterns taking over – after all, this was almost a lifetime of habitual patterns and learnt behaviours on how to cope, I couldn't just switch it off. But I kept coming back. I went through a really challenging time with meditation. After thinking I'd nailed it, finally able to reach a point of stillness within and enjoying my daily practice it then became harder. My concentration shot to pieces by an overwhelming amount of negative self-talk, doubt, judgement. I faced new obstacles, triggering neglect and trust issues, and I felt quite low, I didn't want to sit with the thoughts that were presenting themselves now I'd given them space to show up.

Despite this I still didn't give up, I knew I was on a voyage, one not just to finding myself but to fully arrive back to myself, to where I stand now. I had to encounter a tremendous number of obstacles; it was simply part of it. The more I sat, the more space opened for more to rise and so it continued, and it was uncomfortable at times. Much of the time to be honest. I'm sure I'm really selling this to you! Bear with me!

My daughter wrote a speech on overthinking for an English assignment at school. It was amazing. During her speech she mentioned that it is ten times harder to fix yourself than break yourself. *How true*, I thought, *what about when you don't exactly know which parts are broken or which bits you want to fix?* Ever learning, I realised there were parts of me that I had viewed as broken but were not broken at all, they just didn't fit in with the life I was living. These parts didn't need fixing, they were now points of growth, a new realisation for me. Then there were parts I thought I had nailed but they actually needed fixing the most. The squeezing five hundred tasks into one day, the staying awake at night worrying about what I should have done better, the obsessing over how others saw me, the list goes on.

As time went on, the need to protect myself became stronger, especially with children to look after. Becoming a mum is most certainly one of the greatest and most rewarding adventures of my lifetime so far but for sure the most unpredictable and most challenging too. I am learning all the time. My children too, my teachers.

I remember clear as day, my mum saying to me on more than one occasion how 'Being a parent is the hardest job in the world, nobody trains you for it and you don't know what to expect.'

At the time, I brushed this off with my cocky know-better attitude, feeling hard done by for not being able to stay out later and often thought about all the jobs out there which I thought were much harder than parenting. Now I see what she meant: parenting is a lifelong job with such huge responsibility, and we are winging it, trying our best, then trying to keep up with others, then failing, then winning. It really is a wiggly road. But an unknown ride worth having. Just like this healing journey: unknown, hard to face at times but ever so rewarding along the way. Both opening joy, knowledge, strength and possibility.

I've been told 'respect your elders' on many occasions. I've followed this rule. It's a generational thing, forget about it, and so it goes on. Now – just tipped over my mid-thirties as I write this – I think about this statement as I lie here in my bed at 5am, the only time my writing flows; no distractions, just the birds singing their morning song. I, of course, respect my elders; I also respect my youngers. I feel this common courtesy is a two-way street. I wouldn't walk around thinking I could treat those younger than me with rudeness and disregard with no reason. I recently read a quote, I can't remember it exactly, but it was something like this, 'If you fix yourself, your grandchildren will thank you.' This sat with me for a long while, I thought about it repeatedly. For generations, patterns repeat themselves: anxiety, depression, anger, lack of communication, lack of love, speaking the truth etc. If this could be fixed and addressed somewhere along the line I see it would indeed benefit grandchildren. Their parents, my children, no issues to carry forward. Them free to be themselves. So this is what I aspire to do.

I attended a wonderful retreat recently where a lovely lady said, 'It ran in my family until it ran into me.' Synchronicity struck, again! Reminding me of how important this healing journey truly is, finding those buried parts of ourselves, constantly uncovering them through this work.

I've always been able to have honest, open conversations with my family. At times it has caused problems, other times it has brought us closer. I've watched people close to me suffer dearly because communicating is a real issue, to the point of discomfort, rudeness creeping in and disconnect ever-present.

I began to explore trust. For a while I thought I had issues around it. What did it mean to me? Initially I trusted too easily, learning hard lessons along the way and seeing that life happens to us all. I then turned completely the other way, finding it difficult to trust people at all. This included even my own judgement, so I went along with what I thought fitted in. This became increasingly difficult as I sat in a place of fear and unknowing, discomfort. On rare occasion I began to listen, the intuitive feeling too strong to ignore and with time this grew stronger. It once seemed easier to fit in, to let others lead the way. Far easier to lean into my insecurities as this had become comfortable, I didn't need the battle with myself, what I thought was right versus the 'simple' option of just going along with what suited everyone else. Distrust became embedded as a self-protection mechanism. Ignoring any sense of self-awareness meant I constantly fell in the same trap.

I hadn't realised I was still exploring trust until something happened during a trust exercise on a recent retreat. We were in groups of six. Each person from the group took a turn at going in the centre of the circle. The person in the middle closed their eyes, surrounded by the other five. The idea was to simply start falling in any direction you felt comfortable, but with your eyes closed. The circle then gradually stepped out, increasing the space to fall and thereby for the trust to grow in those around you, supporting you, breaking your fall. My turn came, I was third. There had been two other lovely ladies before me, and three men would go after me. I wasn't expecting what happened at all. I closed my eyes, the circle close round me to start, but I couldn't let go, I couldn't lean into the exercise. A lot became clear for me in this moment as the tears out of nowhere started to stream down my face.

As more tears rose to the surface, the circle held me. I was supported. Despite me not being able to fall, I felt safe enough to let my emotion flow, and they held me. What I had identified when I stepped into the middle was that I was heavier than the two girls before me – this pulled from a stored pattern inside my subconscious mind. With my weight being carelessly commented on in the past at different stages of life by people in the family, I was obviously still carrying some pain here. Additionally, despite the lovely supportive words I heard, I couldn't trust fully. Later that day, I knew what to do: I sat, I waited, I welcomed this invitation to go deeper, I journaled. I saw what past patterns I was holding on to. I found a way to be with this and in turn spoke to another friend in my group. She felt she could let go and trust while inside the circle but didn't feel she could support the person in the middle fully. The whole thing fascinated me. I was solid on the outside, I never doubted myself here, but in the middle I felt lost. We all walk a unique path.

I'm still learning to truly trust myself. Within us if we find a place of stillness, we know what's right, though the search remains ever-present. When uncovering who we are, strength lies within this place and confidence sits here too: trust then rises if we allow. The problem I find is we often don't like the answers our intuition leads to, because it makes us feel uncomfortable. So instead we choose to go along with what appears like the right thing to do, or what others may say as it feels easier. But just for a second, I want to go back to the point my daughter made in her essay: we must remember how much harder it can be to fix yourself than break yourself.

Things manifest and resurface, it's ok to keep doing what we feel is right. This has taken me an exceptionally long time to start accepting. I have always felt that because I've made mistakes that I constantly deserved what I received. I then realised I didn't deserve it all. Now I was finding myself I was determined to come back to this sense of knowing and truly no longer care what others thought: it was what I thought that mattered most in this instance. Deep down I think I'd always known this but I wasn't strong enough to believe in me. To be me.

If you can trust anyone it's you, so cut yourself some slack and listen.

Listening is hard to do if you're anxious, depressed or not with yourself much of the time. Your mind takes over: either you're lost in what's to come or stuck in what has been, so being present with just your own conversation can be a challenge.

I've been in a position many a time when I've needed someone to hear me. Words often tumbling out of my mouth, and my meaning behind them not really understood. This journey teaches me that we must be open with how we feel. I notice since finding myself I am really listening; hearing the spoken words now, reading my own as they come out on the page. I now realise that with what I hear, I can see and understand why a person is the way they are. Silent calls for help sit in our words. Felt in our energy. That expression I've heard so many times now makes sense: 'we have to feel it to heal it'. Being honest so as we are heard and understood. Sure, this isn't easy, but the alternative is remaining lost.

***

So, WHERE DOES mindfulness and meditation fall into this?

Mindfulness is where my journey back to self really began, by gradually practising more and more each day, living mindfully. Meditation has become part of my everyday and I can't emphasise enough that meditating doesn't mean you will have a clear mind. You are simply observing; you are present with what is happening. This why some people enjoy meditative activities such as running, dancing, painting, golf and much more. The key to meditation is coming back to the place of where you are. It's said that we have an average of seventy thousand thoughts each day, so it's impossible not to notice any at all! Our mind will wander, get lost. But the moment you find it's wandered, you're back, you're present. Lost and found, as many times as we need.

What really helped me come back to being mindful each day is the seven attitudes of mindfulness, which are all intertwined and all as equally important. I encourage you to keep these in mind when you make time to listen to yourself (honestly, and without shame). If you're struggling to be present, just feel into which attitude you feel most connected to in that moment and apply this to guiding yourself back. I share with you my own summary and understanding of the attitudes of mindfulness to show how each one individually helps you unravel the layers that build up.

1. Patience

FOR A LONG time, I don't think I had any of this! I would lose patience at work, at home, with my children, in the car. You get where I'm going with this ...

Choosing to live more mindfully and the training I took to become a mindfulness teacher means I am now able to have patience a lot more of the time (not all the time of course – I am only human after all). Having patience prevents you overdoing it and burning out which is all so easy to do.

Being patient is a real gift. It means you no longer rush and miss the moments; you can enjoy every encounter. More than this, however, it means being patient with yourself. My eyes see so much more now I have patience with myself. I enjoy everything so much more. Consequently, my meditation practise has also improved by being a little more patient with myself.

Have patience with yourself today and see what you experience!

2. Non-striving

As CHILDREN, WE are taught 'do your best, try harder'. So the concept of non-striving can be difficult to get your head around.

When meditating, the only goal is to be yourself and pay attention to what's happening. Not striving to be a particular way or get anywhere specific makes this practice easier.

Animals are naturally good at non-striving. They can shift their attention from doing to being. Think how a frog can sit so very still. There are some great mindful exercises showing just this in *Sitting Still Like a Frog: Mindfulness Exercises for Kids (and Their Parents)* by Eline Snel.

3. Non-judging

DON'T FEEL BAD knowing you have judged others in the past.

Our minds are conditioned to put internal experience and feelings into categories. Without even giving it a thought, you may be in a situation, and you've already made a judgement.

- That breakfast you just ate.
- The clothes someone's wearing.
- The evenings getting darker.
- The weather's too cold.
- That person who may not have the same views as you.
- Judging yourself for things you do each day.
- Good/bad, love/ hate, right/wrong, like/dislike etc. ...

Being an impartial witness of your own experience and becoming aware of your judging: this is the practice. If you notice yourself judging just bring yourself back to your awareness or your breath in this present moment, also forgive yourself for it.

Most importantly, give yourself a break of the judgements you make on yourself. You're doing the best you can and that's ok!

4. Trust

TRUST YOURSELF!

Having trust in yourself and others is so important. This can be difficult to do, especially if you have had your trust broken before.

Learning to trust your own experience, feelings and intuition allows for deep self-awareness and acceptance.

Learning to trust others can be a challenge but do try and allow yourself to let the right people in when it feels right.

It's important to trust yourself and your feelings. Spend a little more time with yourself and allow the self-care you deserve. Trust in you and what you need, in time you'll be more accepting of others as well as yourself.

5. Beginner's mind

LEAVING OUR EXPECTATIONS at the door and looking at anything or anyone with fresh eyes gives you a gift. You will see those all too familiar surroundings or people in a new way and may even notice something you've never seen before, even if you've entered that place a thousand times before or been with that person for years on end.

Children naturally possess a beginner's mind as so many things are new to them. As we get older, we lose the ability to see things naturally as our minds are overcrowded with knowledge and experience and we sometimes lose the beauty of 'what is'.

Think of a newborn baby: every time its tiny eyes open, they are full of wonder. Everything is brand new. They look around them moment by moment and take in what's right in front of them, learning each second.

Are you able to do that today?

Look at something familiar as though you don't know anything about it?

Learn something new from this experience?

Open your mind to endless possibilities!

6. Acceptance

ACCEPTING THINGS AS they are, good or bad, enables you to be with whatever's there for you. This sure can be hard to do but there is so much value in this attitude. Don't resist what is already fact. Things will change in their own time – or not change, and that's fine too.

Is there something that's been on your mind recently that you can't escape from but it's not sitting well with you?

Can you try and accept it for what it is? You don't have to like it but what if you try and let it be, even if just for a moment?

7. Letting go

FOR ME THIS is the hardest of the attitudes and needs constant practise but with regular meditation and mindfulness I'm getting there!

Are you able to let go? Or do you hold on to things or feelings you can't change or control? Things that no longer serve you and just take time away from you being able to enjoy this new moment right now.

Try it today: let something go that you may usually hold on to, even something small.

- A car overtaking you on the way to work.
- Your bus being late.
- Forgetting your homework.
- Your child having a meltdown before school.
- Spilling tea in a rush this morning.
- Your laptop freezing so you are unable to connect to that Zoom meeting in time.
- That work taking much longer than you had planned.
- Forgetting your headphones.

Whatever it is for you today, just try if you can (even for a moment) 'letting go' and see how it feels. You can't change it, so just allow yourself to be free from the thought. Even just for a minute. By letting go you may notice something wonderful. If you can't do that, try instead to really hold on to how you feel in that moment and see how that feels for you, in doing so, in time, by learning how you hold on, you will learn how to let go.

8 & 9. Gratitude and generosity

I love these two additional attitudes to mindfulness! They interconnect perfectly with the other seven attitudes, making it easier to encompass all nine together.

Generosity has positive effects on the brain and helps to improve stress and anxiety. Giving your time, knowledge or a gift to somebody without expecting anything back is a wonderful feeling. Also remember to be generous with yourself and take the time you need for you!

Can you give something small to somebody today?

A compliment, a five-minute conversation?

A random act of kindness goes a long way.

Gratitude boosts our mood and improves relationships; it also promotes kindness. People who regularly express gratitude for the positive things in their life are shown to be happier overall, leading to lower rates of stress and depression.

Each day I write down three things I'm grateful for, well most days. It has become a habit, which makes it easier to remember, but of course there are days when it doesn't happen and that's ok, I let it go. We can bring gratitude to anything at all. It could be anything from sunny skies, to nature, my health, my wonderful family. Things we may take for granted, like our sight, love, even our feet that walk us from one place to the next.

What three things are you grateful for today?

***

THESE MINDFUL ATTITUDES can be used each day when doing anything at all; whatever comes up for you try and be mindful. I found adopting this new behaviour started off small, like the tiny moments I suggested above. Gradually, those mindful moments became more frequent, until eventually they were synonymous with (nearly) everything I approached in my everyday life. Trusting myself a little more, letting something go, not judging myself and so much more. Focus on the moments when you can feel your attention shifting. When you become aware of how you feel. When you feel comfortable freeing your emotions. These attitudes formed the basis for much of what needed to change in my life, as you will see in the remaining chapters.

Wait, Surrender

My feet they keep on walking, playing out the
steps.
My mind it tries to rush ahead, I just can't catch
my breath.
Listening and waiting for what I'm meant to do,
My heart it knows the answer, the mind rushing
for the clues.

Stopping, taking rest on a log within the sand,
A voice it whispers quietly, 'Trust the pen within
your hand.'
You're here and waiting solemnly, your eyes are
filled with tears,
Rush forwards all your memories and many
engrained fears.

Holding on to patterns to how life served you
once before,
Inside that sense of knowing, so deep there's
something more.
The doors are open to you now, you just need
to explore,

Be here in this moment, surrender to what has
been,
Meet the good times with the bad, for all you
needed to see.
Make room for every weather, the sun, the wind,
the rain,
Accept the journey, feel it all, surrender once
again.

Your body like the ocean, your heart it's like the
moon,
The sun, the rain, they come and go, don't wish
for them too soon.
Let it unfold beautifully, no attachment to the
time,
For it is just a concept, see beneath the mime.

Surrender to your body, your movement like the
waves,
In this present moment, release the need to crave.
Stop searching for the answers, as in good time
they'll come.
Just breathe, now smile, welcome it all, there is
no need to run.

***

Chapter 4

Wait, Surrender

ON A CONSTANT search for belonging, this race appears to have no finish line. My feet just keep on walking, playing out the steps. Even when I get there, the arrival becomes lost in all that I don't let myself see along the way. We are right here, right now, yet satisfaction in today is often missed.

How often do we take the time to ask ourselves how we are, to enquire with what's really going on inside? Or deeper still, ask ourselves *who* we are? What does this even mean? I have explored this question a multitude of times in the past four years and I never settle on a solid answer. I'm lost in other people's eyes. Each time I ask this question my mind tries to rush ahead, I can't catch my breath.

Meditation is a space where I can be with whatever is present, the unknown, the discomfort, the pain. Beneath all this there is joy and happiness and the answers we seek, too. To find out who we are and what it is we truly need we must wait, listen and surrender just for a little while holding this space for ourselves, to wonder, to explore, to question yet not control what shows up. This can be uncomfortable but it's necessary.

If we don't listen to what we have to say we bury our emotions, our feeling, ourselves. To listen we need silence, and the answers will come.

At times, I still experience frustration in listening and waiting for what I'm meant to do, yet coming back time and time again meant changes started to creep in and it became a little easier each time – and continues to do so even now. It's still never perfect, but I see now the difference, the power in making time, to surrender and wait.

My heart knows the answer, yet my mind is always rushing for the clues. So, I try and remember to just observe.

I was never particularly good at observing, having the tendency to want to get involved and help, give my opinion, take control – of everything! Control is a common coping mechanism for most people (most definitely for me), so being caught up in my head meant I often missed the answers which were lying inside. The same with my thoughts: I wasn't very good at observing them either. My anxiety stemmed from the very need to hold on to every thought. In turn these thoughts would run away with me, taking control. I needed a way to observe my thoughts without them taking hold, so I decided to write.

On a more recent holiday, this really took new meaning for me. For a moment I felt my anxious thoughts returning, my mind racing. I decided to pause. I had recognised the signs. Stopping to take rest, that voice whispered quietly again, *Trust the pen within your hand*. So, I did, I went with it: whatever surfaced I wrote down, the words on the pages didn't seem to make much sense at first, but I began to find meaning. This time that familiar sense of overwhelm didn't take over.

It's not until you learn to observe that you really see how giving attention to your anxious or unwanted thoughts gives them power. Observing is a big part of mindfulness: noticing brings you into contact with your senses and expands your awareness. By observing you can control your attention without clinging on, and spend time with thoughts that are helpful, rather than focusing on anxious or unhelpful thought patterns which distance us from our lives, from this moment.

***

AS A PARENT, I see now I often missed large parts of my own children's birthday parties. I'd spend seventy per cent of the day in the kitchen as I was so busy in the outcome of the day making sure everything played out perfectly. I tried to create moments of joy, rather than just letting them unfold beautifully in the simple pleasures, and even then I missed half of any joyful moments because I was always preoccupied. Now that I pause to observe my breath, my body sensations and sounds – things I never caught sight of before – I am no longer holding on to patterns that served me once before. By connecting with these simple yet missed senses, connecting *inside*, I have that sense of knowing, I can connect deeper; there's something more.

Meditation quiets the mind. It doesn't matter how many times your mind will wander, all you must do is notice and bring your mind back, repeatedly, this giving you a deeper experience in the moment. Allow the thoughts, then silence your judgement of them.

So next time you're buried deep in the kitchen, getting the next part of the perfect day ready, ask yourself, *What's happening in this moment?* Don't miss that first bite of cake smeared over your child's face. Don't miss the start of singing 'Happy Birthday'. Be in the moment, the other moments will still find you; I know which one I'd like to remember.

***

HABITS TAKE HOLD of us all, from time to time: some beneficial and some not so helpful. However, since it takes roughly sixty-six days for a habit to become automatic, if you want to change a habit, or implement a new one, you will need to spend a couple of months on it in order for it to stick. This is why courses in mindfulness are usually over eight weeks – and why many other beneficial health services and courses are offered over a similar period, too. This is so the brain has time to learn the new behavioural patterns which then become natural. Apparently, it's said that we often give up right before we take off, so hang in there and remember, everything takes time. Small changes make a big difference over time.

We go through life trying to fit in, yet rarely surrendering to where we are and how we feel. Pushing down our feelings and desires. Not saying how we feel out of fear and then slipping into a way of being. It may feel safer to hold on to patterns of how life served you once before, but to grow and connect fully to who you are it's important to be aware of the habits which aren't doing you any favours. Often, we don't even realise which bad habits we have embedded, again sucked into keeping up; never pausing for breath we roll into the next day and time slips by. When taking time to observe a little more, rather than be consumed with all the thinking and doing, we get to take in so much more around us and this is where the new habits begin.

Fully embrace the moment every once in a while, and defer the list in your mind.

***

When you let go of what no longer serves you, you create space for what's meant to be. – **Anon**

OUR HABITS AND routines often impede our awareness. I fully believe that what's meant for us won't pass us by but if we don't cultivate moments to connect with ourselves, we end up repeating the same mistakes, encountering the same lesson until we finally give way to the moment, making this space to listen.

Be here in this moment, surrender to what has been, meet the good times with the bad, for all you needed to see. People come into our lives for a little while, some a lifetime and some leave too soon. Without realising, however, we may hold on to people – and other things for that matter – who no longer serve us. This may be out of habit, a sense of obligation or from fear. Remembering that each moment brings us something is an effective way to let go of the attachment and find gratitude in what you have learnt along the way.

Letting go can be difficult, we become comfortable where we are, but it doesn't necessarily mean it's right for us any more and this is tough. We all change, grow and discover ourselves as we move through time. To fulfil all we are meant to be we need to create space and let go along the way. Nature and the weather constantly illustrate this: the continual change and unknown yet beauty and growth forever rising. Make room for every weather: the sun, the wind, the rain; accept your journey, feel it all, surrender once again.

***

WE LIVE IN a fast-paced world, so much to keep up with if we allow. How many times a day are you able to just be? To wait?

We can't fit it all in and some things simply will no longer fit, so choose what's important.

Don't feel bad for doing what you need to do for yourself. Put yourself first. Create some space for what's meant to be.

I can't say it enough: can you simply, just be? So simple, yet so powerful. For when we do, the doing takes care of itself!

Overthinking and wanting more are two things we all easily get consumed by. More often than not, allowing yourself time out from all the things outside of today can be harder for us to embrace than the constant rush we often experience regularly.

Wouldn't it be nice to enjoy being for a bit? Feeling the experience we're in. 'Doing' all the time is exhausting. Explore taking a moment to surrender and see how that feels. Feel the freedom in it.

If you struggle with being present and slowing down, mindfulness and meditation can really help with this. Remember the mindful attitudes: have a little patience and let go, if even just for a moment. Bringing awareness to the present moment allows you to fully engage and feel the joy in being. Returning your attention to this moment, however many times you need to, enables you to not get caught up in anything that has already happened nor all the other things that haven't happened yet.

I have noticed during winter that snow enables many of us to become a little more mindful, even if it's something not usually practised. Heavy snowfall stops what you possibly should have been doing in its tracks, helping you experience the moment for what it is. Embracing the snow, slowing down and just being as the rush isn't possible. Getting outside, sledding, playing and feeling the snow. Being fully emerged in the here and now, feeling all the wonder in this unplanned, joyous moment. A sudden stop, a calm, feeling alive, everything else has to wait. We too can choose this every now and then, without waiting for any snowflakes.

***

I HAVE TWO dogs and they provide the most non-judgemental, pure love every time I walk through the door. They don't have the same attachment to time and when they hear the key in the door their happy, excited reception greets me every time. I smile as I see how happy they are. Pure love, not attached to any fallout from yesterday. Nor what's to come tomorrow. Nothing clouding the feelings felt, nor changing to fit in; simply showing up. They move mindfully throughout the day, they feel the moment, then the next one. I learn from them every day observing the moments when they simply pause, seeing them just curled up, taking rest. When they need it, they just stop. Of course, I am aware they don't go to work etc., but the lessons here remind me what's important amongst it all. Tuning into what feels right rather than holding on to what you feel is expected.

***

TRY TO CREATE moments where you don't have to rush for what's to come. The freedom felt when not watching the clock, no concept of time even for a while lifts the pressure and gives you a chance to just be.

We can spend so much time looking forward, waiting for what's next that we often miss much of today. While it is of course nice to look forward to things, we don't want to get so caught up in the future that we are always chasing what we think we need for fulfilment.

Going forward I try, the best I can, to spend each day as it comes. Not worrying about the day just gone or the day to come. If the pandemic we have lived through has taught me anything, it was to appreciate and slow down a little, to notice. Don't get lost and let fear take you off track: trust your intuition and find your way back.

Later will come in its own time, but we have so much to enjoy right now – see it and feel it.

Take a moment and look at all you have, all that is around you and smile. Be grateful for what is here in this moment. Breathe it in.

The moment we have, this second, is so precious and like no other.

***

Sometimes doing nothing is the most daring move of all. – **Jeff Warren**

AT TIMES WE drift so easily, yet at others a barricade of rocks blocks the natural flow. I have found that doing nothing really is a challenge, I become my own obstruction to surrender. I fill the pauses with noise, leading me into the fire until I burn out.

Looking back, the moment when I understood this quote was a transformational point. On this occasion, this realisation, I had no choice but to stop and revisit myself. I delved in and set myself a challenge to at times, do nothing! Reminded, the lesson keeps coming until you listen. This is something I now fully understand as I have recently revisited many of the same lessons, pulled to revisit challenges, yet now from a place of strength inside. It seems such a simple thing, doesn't it? Be who you are, slow down, take a break! I keep saying it throughout, but we forget. Often, we are hidden beneath so many versions of what we think we should be or need to be to fit in we lose ourselves by trying to keep up ... it's flipping exhausting!

I have now learnt to be me, see me, and do nothing from time to time. Until you can sit, be yourself and stop reaching, you don't see what you already have.

I was looking at 'stuff' all the time but never actually seeing it clearly for what it actually was. I was listening but not hearing.

Sometimes we don't want to stop, we don't want to face what's there, which is half the battle, ultimately resulting in not getting to this point quicker. We'd rather not face the deep hidden wounds, the unopened jars. Those lids tightly on.

***

SOMETIMES WE CREATE distractions, keeping ourselves busy to avoid other things which we'd rather not face, for me – my anxiety.

You may think stopping is wasting your time, because you have so much to do! But to stop and do nothing, contemplation, meditation, possibly facing things you are avoiding is the most daring move of all, a big step for some. It can also be the most enlightening.

By doing nothing during meditation I see I can feel freedom, equanimity. When feeling anxious this can be really challenging but I'm realising it's ok to have choiceless awareness, not always thinking and doing – this is freeing for my mind. Eventually, the draining feeling of always doing got far too much.

Doing something for yourself and taking time to stop is needed, it doesn't mean you care any less it just means you are finding balance. There will always be some people, some jobs that will keep taking, always expecting more of you – if you allow it. The responsibility of not being taken advantage of is yours. If you don't give yourself permission to stop, you won't.

Saying no is an absolute must sometimes. You need to stop and make time for you. Create your path, fill some of your time with what you enjoy, your passions and don't feel guilty for it. Who are you, what do you like, what do you want?

Being present with ourselves and not getting caught up in all the 'should haves' and 'must dos' allows you to stop and take a breath, a moment for you.

Looking back, the only person stopping me having time for me, being me, was me! Stop searching for the answers, as in good time they'll come. Just breathe, now smile, welcome it all, there is no need to run.

Anxiety

Embrace the unknown.
Why do we so often fear what is to come?
Anxiety rising once more like the sun.
It takes over, its presence, the fear kicking in,
Something unsettled felt deep within.

Anxiety emerging, the thoughts consume my head,
Will somebody please help me put them back
to bed?
My mind it wants to follow, the thoughts in size
they grow,
Conclusions, endless outcomes, the seeds that
I sow.

Beneath all the anxiety lays the trauma that I shield,
Yet unable to bare it and expose like an open field.
Why do I avoid it? Running from the pain,
Sitting with anxiety seems easier than shame.

When brave enough to feel it, lessons I am shown,
The anxiety it softens, habitual patterns thrown.
I stop make time to listen, I see now what is here,
Right in this moment, there is nothing to fear.

The anxiety it rises, once more like the sun,
But this time I see that I don't need to run.
I step back in awareness, now I clearly see,
The light shining brightly, into my soul, into me.

No longer wrapped in stories, the ones that I once fed,
Or the heartache, the torture, the memories I'd once dread.
Each of those moments led me to today,
Then came love and acceptance; a new, open way.

***

Chapter 5

Anxiety

I THOUGHT I was getting there, but today I feel stuck!

I've worked hard to overcome my anxiety. Through mindfulness and meditation I've found balance and healthier coping techniques. Much of the time my days are no longer consumed by old patterns. Mindfulness has also enabled me to sit with the uncomfortable and befriend my experience whatever it may be, each time getting a little better.

I have learnt so many insightful things. Some days I am able to channel everything into what I believe in, giving myself more time, being kinder to myself and appreciating all I have. I am so grateful for everything I have and the experience that led me here, each piece of the puzzle hugely important. Mid-panic attack you wouldn't find me reaching for the gratitude if I'm honest, for me I found this almost impossible, but living with far less anxiety means I can now see the growth, the realisations. But there are still days when I feel stuck, despite the growth and positive steps taken. This happened for me recently; out of the blue it pops up,

I feel worried, I doubt myself. Then I feel upset at myself for feeling this way, a constant battle of getting lost then finding my way – lost and found once more but it is part of the healing and, like everything else, we come through it. I remind myself, it doesn't take away all the progress made, it doesn't take away what's still achievable and most importantly a day of feeling stuck doesn't mean you are back to square one, you just need to take a step back and allow a different perspective so you can take the next step with wider eyes.

Even as I write this, I feel better, writing and journaling playing a huge part of processing my feelings, knowing the page always listens, non-judgementally.

If you're feeling stuck, fed up, anxious or whatever it may be for you, allow yourself to feel this way for a bit, it's natural. It's just an off day and we all have these. In no time at all things will change, they always do. But the change is far easier when you allow space for it to be present. A natural progression, no resistance. These moments just help us grow each day a little stronger, this off day is all part of that, now showing you how capable you are: you can get through anything! I've become ok with sitting with how I feel and letting these feelings pass through in their own time. By holding the space, they move through far easier.

***

Mindfulness, meditation and writing have transformed me; the way I show up, the way I manage, the way I process. The route I take always comes back to love. The fear takes me away, but if you don't feel worthy of love, the way back to it is distant. Of course, even now, the odd little worry occasionally creeps in, but I can allow it, observe it and let go. More importantly I notice my thoughts around this. Each time it passes a little quicker and sometimes I don't have any concern for the twinges I feel in my body or about my health at all – which for me is such a big transformation. I am lucky to have found support and through the work I now do I have built a network where openly talking about anxiety and all things usually pushed aside is now quite normal. It reminds me to take each day moment by moment and continue to unfold as I go.

Never suffer alone as you can overcome everything. You are here reading this, aren't you? That in itself shows you are still going, still looking for the right thing for you and open to wanting to do the work.

***

Anxiety and me

ANXIETY HAS BEEN a huge part of my life. It took me away from myself, but gaining control over it also led me back to where I am today, creating new parts of me, now inspired to help others. I have a better understanding of who I am and what anxiety is. I am grateful for my journey just as it is – without it I wouldn't have had the experiences which led me to this very moment.

Instead of ignoring anxiety, I eventually confronted it.

I discovered there are so many overlapping elements of anxiety: thoughts, overthinking, fear, worry, repeated patterns. By learning what contributes to anxious thoughts and feelings I finally understood how to release them from my life. Anxious thoughts and fear intersect across several channels, which you will see reflected in this chapter as I take you through the various overlapping twists and turns it takes for anxiety to form and grow, and how I created a route to release anxiety from my life.

Anxiety is not pleasant; we all experience a natural amount of worry throughout life but unless you've lived under the dark cloud of fear you may not fully understand how severe an anxiety disorder can be. A natural response to someone expressing their worries is often 'Don't worry'. The thing is, you can't just 'stop worrying' or 'snap out of it'. This sense of worry is pervasive. You're not having an off day. Anxiety disorders affect many people and it's important that we understand how real this is. Fears and worries begin to take over, seeming out of proportion, but living in this way is truly exhausting. It is hard to take back control and separate reality from fear.

Suffering with anxious thoughts is disabling in many ways, it prevents you from doing many things you actually *want* to do, but you're held back as you feel frightened. Some days just getting out of bed seems scary and unmanageable. Anxiety causes physical symptoms in the body because of the thought patterns in the mind. The feelings that come with an anxiety disorder can be extraordinarily strong.

I feel truly lucky, after suffering with health anxiety and panic for nearly two decades, I now have a greater understanding and the awareness to not get lost in this way of thinking and living any more. It's taken time to unravel but I did it and it is possible for us all to do the same. I've worked through a lot of traumas and uncovered an immense amount of pain along the way. I have also tried numerous therapies. Some of which didn't work for me but may work well for someone else and this is the thing: finding your own way. There is always a way, it's just discovering it that can be tricky, but the route to this point is so important. Where I sit today, I feel the difference, my family sees the difference in me too.

***

YOU MAY HAVE read *The Power of Now* by Eckhart Tolle. He also authored a lovely book called *Milton's Secret*. Both highlight the importance of living in the present moment, delivering a message, one I have learnt to adopt when I can.

As someone who has suffered with anxiety, worry would constantly fill my mind – this isn't healthy. Of course, we all worry at some point, but I was spending so much time worrying about things I had no control over, creating pressure which manifested into bouts of fear. After much self-discovery, reading, practise and time I now see the only thing I have power over is 'Now'. I still wonder, but in a healthier way.

When this lesson is learnt, it seems both too simple and impossible not to constantly plan. 'What do I do without a plan?' However, simply by being present you remove many problems straightaway … after all they aren't here! We are never actually there; in the event we spend so much time overthinking. You miss so much with the rushing, craving the next thing, the constant need to keep up.

Living in thoughts of the future became a coping technique to try and prevent anything bad happening, to avoid facing things – but it didn't work. I worried and then planned, trying to feel like I was on top, but the truth is, I was drowning beneath it all. If this time has taught me anything it's that 'Now' is the only certainty we have, it's ours to enjoy. Planning to some degree is part of life for us all and useful in areas but not to excess; there's no need.

***

Your body is your first home. – **Martha Graham**

WHEN EXPERIENCING MENTAL health issues, it is normal to feel trapped. Thoughts arise: *I need to get out of here, I must go out to feel better ... book a holiday ... find a distraction*, or alternatively not want to move at all, overwhelmed completely. The thing is, the place where you are trapped sits in the mind – unanswered questions, unresolved problems – discomfort then presents in your body; all a natural response to stress and fear. The flip side is to feel trapped inside your body, again this usually starting in the mind. To be able to observe this and notice this is something you *feel*, rather than identifying it as what you *are* is so important. Your response will then become far more helpful, and healthier!

To feel truly at home, comfortable and not confined in this way you need to make peace with yourself. Heal your mind and your body: connect. Looking after your body is important, it carries you through this life but sometimes it can be a challenge. When you make space to see what's present in your mind, the healing happens, which in turn heals your body. Positive thoughts follow and motivation to look after yourself comes organically. If you step out of your head and listen to your heart, if you love yourself and feel content within, even if you are facing difficulties then you can feel at home wherever you go.

Jon Kabat-Zinn states: 'Wherever you go, there you are.' If you can find happiness in the present moment and make it a way to live your life, it can be found every day in all you do. You won't feel trapped, and you will be able to enjoy what you have and with each breath appreciate every new moment, including the sad ones. When this begins to happen for you, all the holidays, adventures and outings you once sought as a means of escape will become pure enjoyment for what they are, not a place to hide away.

Too often we hold on to what is to come and miss today, then when we get to where we thought escape was, we end up searching for something else. Freedom is a state of mind. True happiness and peace are found within you. Once discovered, everything you see is beautiful in some way; it's growth.

***

LOCKDOWN REALLY TOOK its toll on the world in so many ways, much of it unseen or not spoken about and this unravelled each day that went by for us all: the lessons, changes, priorities, the questions. I knew I was blessed; my family were coping well. Both my daughters loved their six-month home straight stint! I, on the other hand, cracked at week nine. I'd painted, I'd walked everywhere, I'd baked, tidied, sorted, crafted. Watched movies, played cards, board games, gone on bike rides. There was only so much that could distract me from myself! I'd done what I could, and (I don't want to sound ungrateful) it all just became so monotonous! I used to think it was work, dance runs, school drop offs, pick-ups that were the problem, but it appeared whatever become routine for too long got on my nerves, yet I also wanted it to keep going, to keep busy. I gained a lot during this time – both in the spiritual sense and a literal heaviness as baking became a regular hobby! It was like therapy, making meringues; the clear egg white transforming into an airy foam and then when the sugar went in, seeing it slowly swirl into a fluffy foam, thickening into this glossy, heavenly, picturesque snow. I wanted to jump into the bowl and ski around the swirls; it looked so inviting!

I kept going with the distractions but then often started feeling quite angry. I just wanted a bath on my own! No interruptions, just a bath! Was I that bad a teenager that I was not able to have a thirty-minute bath by myself?! I would often flash back to my troubled younger self and assess if this was some kind of karma (now having a deeper understanding of karma I know differently, but it didn't stop the recurring thoughts at the time). In this particular moment would I get the peace? Clearly not, I get in and fifteen minutes later my youngest daughter (at this point only seven) is at the door, then coming in and sitting on the toilet. 'I can't sleep,' she says. Bless her but FUCK! One bath in peace, I don't want to win the lottery (well I wouldn't say no …) but just a bath! Please!

Anyway, that evening I snapped; I knew it was coming. I couldn't sleep, I went straight to bed after my interrupted bath, no energy to even watch the once much-loved TV! I drifted off but an hour later I was bolted awake in fear, a heavy feeling in my chest, my legs felt dead. I tried to drift off, but it kept happening. Straight on Google. *Am I having a heart attack? Am I dying, do I have a blood clot, kidney failure?* I'm not sure which but I felt awful. I wanted to sleep so badly but couldn't. Almost on the hour every hour the same thing was happening. *Shit, what's wrong with me, is it anxiety or is this really it?* I am googling for reassurance, though it doesn't help, it just makes everything worse. I listen to Audible, some calming music, I try and meditate. *Augh! Nothing is working!* I cry again and with exhaustion finally drift off for a few hours. When I wake again, daylight present, I felt like I've been hit by a truck, but I'm alive.

My fear softened; I gave myself a reminder that my anxiety is always health-based. Anything to do with my body or health a major concern for me. Just being able to recognise this filled me with emotion; it was a real revelation. I was, day by day, becoming more aware. I wasn't living in fear any more – I was living. Of course, I still *felt* anxious, but I wasn't anxiety!

Take it from someone who thought this would never happen … years on and these days I can untangle a situation like this quite quickly. I am free from this. Meditation, writing and mindfulness created the foundation for this freedom.

***

What mental health needs is more sunlight, more candour, and more unashamed conversation. – **Glenn Close**

A LOT OF my self-discovery has been through reading something I feel connected to – as you can see throughout this chapter. I don't just read a quote: I really explore its meaning to me, and through this I uncover a little more. I've been writing and thinking a lot about this quote, with it being so close to my heart.

Why are so many people struggling? Is it because for a long time mental health wasn't as talked about, seen as a problem? Or because, like many things, because it's not a visible wound, it's pushed aside?

It is perfectly ok to have a mental health issue, to talk about it, to be truthful with those around you and to allow yourself to process this with kindness, no shame and plenty of warmth.

We should never feel we need to hide a mental health issue, just as we wouldn't hide a broken leg. Parts of us don't effectively work all the time, this is part of being alive. We each have flaws which make us – us! They make us beautiful, unique and strong in our own way.

Living through severe anxiety and having family members who have also suffered with their mental health I see these challenges that arise for us as a point of growth.

Mental health issues present as a warning, a sign to work on something, something inside that needs attention. But because it isn't visible, and the unnecessary stigma attached to it, we put it off and push it aside. We feel ashamed or embarrassed. It becomes an unspoken topic left to brew.

Rest, take some time out. Seek help if you need to, talk truthfully, don't suffer alone, no problem is too small. Make space to heal – just as you would with a broken bone. Allow the sun to shine on you, be seen and heard. It is ok to ask for help: there is help available so please share your struggles.

Sometimes you just need to hear … You're not the only one!

How true this is – well it is for me anyway!

I suffered with health anxiety for a long time. Worrying constantly about every little pain, too much time on Google, constantly asking for reassurance.

Mindfulness and meditation really helped me work through this. I am now able to be present and focus on what I already have – not what's next, or that what ifs, which rarely happen anyway. The more I discover, the more I see it really is about the moment you are in now. That's what is fact, that's what you have right now. Do you ever get to the goal anyway? When you arrive, there is always something else to get to.

By not worrying about things to come and what could be I can now separate my thoughts from who I am. This doesn't take away the fact that I do feel anxious occasionally and have moments of worry here and there.

Previously, however, when anxious I would always seek reassurance from somebody. Have they felt this pain? Do they know what I mean? Knowing you're not the only one is reassuring and helps you feel at ease.

Sometimes all you need to hear is, you're not the only one who …

- Has ever suffered with anxiety.
- Hasn't revised for that test.
- Couldn't get out of bed in the morning.
- Was running late for school pick up.
- Just simply couldn't be bothered.
- Missed a deadline.

It's ok to want support, to reach out for reassurance or help; it always feels better knowing you are not alone. I heard this again recently when listening to *Living With Intention*, it shows everybody feels this way at some point – even if they seem like they've got it all together.

You're not alone in how you feel, or with mistakes you have made. Nobody is perfect and that's how it should be. Just know – you are not the only one and remember that asking for help is brave. The more we openly speak up, that ripple spreads and others feel safe to do the same.

***

EVEN WHEN THINGS feel incredibly dark, the light still shines below it all. I always remember that famous quote in Harry Potter when Dumbledore reminds us to flick on our own switch in times of darkness.

Do you ever lie there at night, thoughts going round in your head?

Why is anxiety always worse in the dark of the night? The worries seem unbeatable, the thoughts irrational, it can be a lonely place.

We know the brain doesn't fully switch off when we are sleeping so when you get into bed in the dark of the night things come to the forefront of your mind with no distractions. These thought patterns you have in place intensify things to get worse, so by changing the patterns the thoughts will soon change too.

Can you remember to turn on your light?

Turning on the light for you can be your way to bring happiness to your bedtime routine alleviating some of those thoughts.

- Run a nice bath.
- Do a bedtime meditation.
- Read a book.
- Listen to some music.
- Write in your journal.

Whatever works for you, if your anxiety worsens at

night-time then try something new, don't lie there feeling worse for hours on end. I know how that feels.

If you can, just allow your feelings to be seen, even if just for a moment.

If you can't sleep, remember to turn on your light and feel a bit of happiness even in the dark of the night. By doing this and creating bedtime comforts, you will guide yourself to fewer worries and a better sleep.

Mindfulness practices can help you to increase your ability to regulate emotions, decrease stress, anxiety and depression.

Mindfulness and meditation firstly improved my sleep, I sleep now! Yes, actually sleep! This was a great start for me as I had so much more energy and was able to focus. I started to feel good about myself, upbeat for everything, being alive, even the grey sky out the window! Until this change, I thought I felt better in the sunshine but what I finally realised was that I could feel great on a grey day, too. I could finally be myself, the person I'd always been but for so long had not let myself due to constant judgement, social pressures to fit in and my own criticism and fears. Finally, I was starting to let all of this go. With more energy to face everyday tasks, I had the mental capacity to start letting go. Of course, as I've said, anxiety can still creep in, I get lost in thought as we all do but I can now catch myself a little earlier and bring myself back.

I reach for the pen and journal once more, stop and notice my breath – even if just one – and appreciate that in itself. In time the gratitude for living just started coming.

It hasn't always been this way, however. A note I wrote one day surprised me recently as I reread an old journal:

Gosh, it was a beautiful day; the sun was warming my skin, prickling in the hazy heat. Walking round the open fields, dogs running through the long grass, I felt free and uplifted but all so quickly that feeling just changed. The fear set in again and I couldn't shake it. It didn't matter what I felt but I would obsess over it. That burning in my tummy, the ache in my shoulder, a tingle in my hand. It started to take over, it was affecting my daily life. The children were affected, my work was affected, and it was draining. My fight-or-flight response was permanently switched on and I didn't know how to get a handle on it and switch it off. I should be enjoying this time, but I simply couldn't fully. I get home and try to support some sort of focus yet find myself reaching for another biscuit – even though I'm not even hungry – to mask the unpleasant background feeling deep inside me. This was becoming a regular thing, the biscuit munching; they were calling me from the cupboard as I walked through to put the washing on! No chance of a body transforming supermodel appearing from this house after lockdown! As I scroll through Instagram posts of beauties keeping fit, trialling new make-up regimes and skincare products. I was delighted that I made lunch for everyone, got dressed `and washed my hair without cracking up.`

Reflecting on this really stopped me in my tracks. Now I can see how, little by little, my transformation had been huge yet all the while in it I was beating myself up for once more not doing enough, not being enough. Never stopping to see how far I'd come. We are all guilty of this and find it easier to put ourselves down rather than lift ourselves up.

***

Why worry?

PLENTY OF TIME is spent worrying about almost everything you can think of at some stage. Many of these thoughts sit in comparison and judgement. Why do we spend so much time worrying about what others think? Ultimately, it's what holds us back. It delays us moving forward and stepping into all we are capable of. The fear of other people's thoughts and opinions making us question and veer away from the gut instinct that keeps rising.

Trying to fit in, say the right thing or say nothing at all for the fear of what others think – essentially living in other people's heads, not our own. Worried about what we wear … how we come across … if I say something, is it wrong? Will people think I'm stupid? This list is endless: how draining all of this is! So much time wasted as we try to fit in, so we don't get cast aside, left out, the fear of missing something. I have spent so much time worrying about what people think about me, what they might say.

Why does it matter what others think? But here's the thing: it doesn't have to if you don't want it to! We just get sucked into this, others then seemingly having power of our own thoughts. I'm always telling my children they can be anything they want to be, do anything they want to do, so why do I fear what people will say if I try the same thing?

I have now finally realised, we will never please everyone. There will always be someone who will pass judgement. It's now apparent, the most important person's opinion of me, the one that really matters – is my own! That's where all the judgements can take over. It's also where they can stop.

I'm allowing myself to be more like the birds: not worrying about what others think or hear, gaining confidence along the way and believing I can achieve my dreams.

Thoughts don't define who you are or what you can do. We have ownership over our feelings, too. If we are true to ourselves, that's what matters. I hope you too can be true to yourself – fulfil all your dreams, don't let other thoughts stand in your way.

***

My life has been full of terrible misfortunes most of which never happened. – **Michel de Montaigne**

WHEN READING THIS quote, we will each take our own message from it and interpret it in different ways. For me it's so relatable to my struggle with anxiety over the years.

I have spent a lot of time consumed with worry, fear of what's to come, what might happen to me, my loved ones. Of course, we have all lived our own misfortunes and worries in our lifetime but filling your day with these thoughts and worrying to excess about things that haven't even happened yet isn't healthy.

The more I practise mindfulness and meditation, being fully in the present moment I see all the energy I wasted. Anxiety largely had me living in the future: thinking, worrying, fearing what may or may not happen taking away full enjoyment at times. It was truly exhausting. I am grateful, as now I feel this way far less – in fact hardly ever at all – but when I notice the feeling of anxiety now, I recall that exhaustion and also remember how, more often than not, ninety-nine per cent of the time all those worries I feared would happen were never actually realised.

Now I can read this quote and recognise how I became lost in worry. Hours and hours consumed with fearing events or scenarios that never happened. I was addicted to trying to protect myself, to gain control by putting up a protective barrier. I thought if I could think through and google every outcome (including the worst), I would be able to prevent everything. But this doesn't work, it just steals time. Anxiety and fear taking away from what you can genuinely enjoy today. Now when I catch myself running away with these feelings, I notice them and acknowledge them; a simple act serving as a gentle reminder to come back.

I know you can't just snap out of feeling anxious, and others not experiencing fear, panic attacks or anxiety on a high level may expect you to just 'get a grip' or 'stop worrying' but this takes time and requires space.

It took me a long time to learn how to manage my own anxiety. One thing that stands out from my experience is that you will only do it in your own time. The thing that held me back was not allowing myself the time to break my anxious habits. I was even scared to do this; I knew what to expect when anxiety rose, the loop I would initiate and it was easier to fall back into these patterns than digging deeper.

So please, take the time you need, give yourself that time. Then you can spend less time worrying and more time in a life where you enjoy what is happening.

***

The flow of fear

HAVE YOU EVER felt that deep sense of fear?

For some of us, a constant flow of fear is too easily accessible. We seem to effortlessly get consumed by it, in turn making it harder to detach from fear. If we allow it, fear becomes present, rises inside and takes over.

Fear was the main culprit of my health anxiety, taking over most days. Fear is such a powerful emotion and can have a huge effect on the mind and body. With my anxiety, I thought building up all this fear was keeping me safe. It wasn't. It doesn't.

It's likely you have felt fear on some level. Fear of an upcoming test or exam, a job interview. Fear of the unknown, of what's to come. Fear following trauma. On top of our own daily pressures and natural anxieties the constant fear the media imparts doesn't help. Sometimes the cup overflows, and fear takes over. But it doesn't always have to feel this way.

A persistent feeling of fear is an overwhelming place to be. Feeling frightened all the time, it consumes you and stops you being.

The important thing to remember is that we *feel* fear; we are not fear.

Fear is an emotional response to a definite threat. When you suffer with anxiety, however, you feel under threat much of the time, creating a fear of whatever it is you're anxious about. This may be health anxiety, social anxiety, specific phobias. Eventually, fear can cause anxiety, and anxiety can cause fear. Fear can seem everlasting if not managed.

The good news is you can overcome this immense fear. With practice we can manage our feelings and thoughts. Mindfulness and meditation have enabled me to work through this and sit with these feelings; in time being able to see the thoughts rather than allow them to consume me. I now know I am not those feelings of fear, and they don't need to stay long term.

We know that what we pay attention to grows. But remember, our minds are so powerful, we can choose what we focus on. When feeling fearful, you focus on this emotion, the panic, thus in turn generating more fear and anxiety. Then more anxiety and fear … you see the pattern. When overwhelmed you can't differentiate between the feeling and the thought. By slowing down, meditating, it helps you watch these thoughts instead, it's quite amazing.

If you can face your fears, even challenge them a little, it really does give them less power. Question your worst fear: what's the worst that can happen? Has it? Do you feel as afraid?

When we sit in fear, to some extent we have already lost. The fear prolongs any actual or anticipated pain. The mind takes over and presents its own problems. My dog recently had a fairly major operation and beautifully exemplified how mindful animals are and the difference that can be made when only living in the present. During his recovery, I could see there was no fear present. Because he rested, sat with it and listened to his body, when the physical healing had taken its course, he was fighting fit with no after-effects. I think mainly because there was no fear to prolong his recovery time.

By removing the fear, you can enjoy the moment. This one! Allow yourself that pocket of freedom amongst it all; you owe it to yourself.

***

Anxious patterns

WHY DO THE patterns of anxiety repeat themselves again and again?

Suffering with anxiety is dreadful. For those of you who have experienced anxiety on a severe scale (beyond minor anxious patterns) you will already understand how awful this can be and the extreme fear that is felt. Living under this cloud, full enjoyment of your life is dimmed. Feeling trapped within your own mind, constantly worrying about what's to come, it's truly exhausting.

The reason we get caught in this loop is because we give our thoughts power. Feeding the thoughts produces more thoughts, then more after that and the cycle continues. To break this cycle, we must learn that we are not the thoughts and fears in our minds. Instead, we need to learn to observe them – that is the way out from this.

The reason mindfulness and meditation is a proven tool to help overcome anxiety, depression and much more is because they help us to create the distance essential to allow us to separate ourselves from our thoughts and simply observe them. Over time, you will begin to see small subtle changes. You will become present day to day and find you are no longer living in the thoughts, instead you are just living. Once you realise this is possible and that you can indeed step back, things inside begin to change. You will begin to understand and embrace, rather than predict an unlikely future.

Enjoyment of all things, without fear or gloom hanging over your head, *is* possible. The time to make the change is now. Just remember the smallest changes often have the biggest impact and we won't all do things in the same way or at the same speed.

When we have a scenario, a problem or a mental health issue, we need to find the right solution that works for us. It may take time to discover the right fit but there is always a way through. Doing things differently to somebody else isn't wrong, it's simply a route, a solution that works best with what you need.

We all respond differently in situations, throughout life; the good news is we have the power to choose how we respond. While we can't control every situation that arises for us, how we choose to respond will make all the difference. Don't feel you need to react the same way as everyone else, do so in a way that feels right. Choose responses that are healthy for you.

***

WE PLAN SO much, we live in our heads, but we mustn't forget to live …

It's good to have dreams but it is also important not to spend all our time on what could have been or what's yet to come. Dwelling on what might have been in the past or what could be in the future distracts us from living in the present moment. When present, you find yourself here – now. In this moment. This one! Fully immerse yourself in it!

It's not always that easy though, is it? I lived for a very long time lost in feelings of anxiety and with this came an immense amount of overthinking, blocking the simplicity of feeling pockets of happiness and noticing the present moment was nearly always impossible.

Why do we believe our thoughts and get stuck in this cycle of overthinking? It's natural to get caught up in those daily thoughts – all seventy thousand of them! But when we *attach* to those thoughts, we give them power and the cycle of overthinking continues.

Erma Bombeck said that 'overthinking is like a rocking chair, it gives you something to do but doesn't get you anywhere.' Yet our energy follows our thoughts, so when stuck inside this thought process, the loop can be hard to break, but it is possible. Finding your way back to you is hard work and it starts with diving deep inside the layers you've formed to get by; each one a coping mechanism driving you to where you are today. You've simply created a habit where you begin to predict what will happen, but remember you can't actually know this. It's difficult to break down the walls but think of this African proverb: 'if there is no enemy within, the enemy on the outside can do us no harm.' So, it's worth it, trust me and more importantly, trust yourself!

***

ONE OF THE biggest powers we have is to not react to things, if we are able to observe and not jump in, we have more control over everything.

I have shared my struggle with health anxiety and through this battle my thoughts would constantly take control of my mind, my attention giving them power to control my entire day. When I allow them to be without reaction they do pass by and are powerless. If I give power to my thoughts it just takes away all the enjoyment I could have in today.

Reacting to things can cause unnecessary pain and wastes time. If you take a moment and allow your thoughts to just be, changing your response to just sit, you can be still with this.

***

Get out of your thoughts and into your feelings!

SOUNDS SIMPLE, BUT it can be exceedingly difficult to do. Yet such great advice. We know we can't have a completely clear mind; thoughts will come. Anxiety or not, everyone has numerous thoughts, sometimes far too many of them clouding up reality, making it difficult to focus. This one line really brings me back into my body.

Giving unwanted or intrusive thoughts more attention allows them to become bigger. However, we need to ensure we don't force these thoughts away, either.

I've learnt that it's also ok for our thoughts to be with us for a moment. In that moment, shift your awareness and attention to how you actually *feel* when these thoughts pop up, instead of ruminating on what those thoughts could mean or how they might play out.

As a thought emerges, rather than pay 'it' attention, divert your awareness to any sensation you have in your body instead. Play with this in your mind. How does your breathing feel? You might have cold fingers; how does that feel? You might have tingling in your feet or a rumble in your tummy (are you simply hungry?). By focusing on these feelings instead of paying too much attention to our thoughts it snaps you out of it, even if just for a moment.

The key is to just keep noticing, and when you do, you've got it. That's it, just notice when you're lost and in that split second, you're found.

When those thoughts arise, feel them, see them, hold them and let them move through. For when we do, when we stop and notice our breath, when we listen to what we need, little pockets of freedom follow. Now you have given the feeling some space, the emotions attached to them have room to rise. In turn, a diversion naturally presents itself and that thought floats away on its own.

After practising this for a little while, I found that moment of diverted attention and focus on my feelings would get longer, and the curiosity of those feelings would pleasantly take over. Paying mindful attention to these feelings even became fascinating! Cutting those unwanted thoughts off from the attention they don't need means they have no cause to linger as they did before.

If they still take hold, that's the time to really hold on. In time you will learn to let go. There are lots of little tips within this book to help you try different things, and some will be more effective for you than others.

Come back to the journaling, use the letting go meditation on page 310, make time to explore.

Try stopping whatever you are doing right now to focus and observe (even reading this page). Sit still and be with what is.

Try giving each thought a colour and see how your mind attaches to this instead.

***

And finally, on thoughts, always remember this: 'you are not your thoughts'.

Whatever your thoughts are for you today, especially if they feel a bit overwhelming – just remember that's not who you are. Without reaction your thoughts are powerless.

Whatever your thoughts are today, just know that, like the weather, they will change. They always pass.

***

Calm, balance, ease, stillness and peace

I have been listening to quite a few of Jay Shetty's meditations recently. During the meditations he often asks you to bring your awareness back to calm, balance, ease, stillness, and peace. If I can't bring myself to the calm or the balance straightaway I can usually start to do so by the ease or stillness. It reminds me to bring myself back no matter how much my mind wanders.

Meditation really is wonderful and particularly helpful for

managing anxious thoughts. You don't need to get anywhere or reach a 'floaty state' with a completely clear mind, legs crossed. You just need to explore and find the right meditation techniques that work for you, that fit with you.

The interpretation of meditation isn't always accurate, and often defers people from trying. When discussing meditation with people who haven't tried it before, they often think they do not have enough time or that they are doing it wrong.

Meditating is bringing your attention to the world around you, and more than this, the world inside you. You can do this anywhere, for as long or short as you feel comfortable. It can be so accessible if you don't get caught up on what should be. There are of course benefits of spending longer periods of time meditating but taking control of your mind so you can focus and find some stillness in your day is what it's all about.

When meditating you are watching your thoughts, bringing awareness to them. This simple step means you are not lost in them. It is the noticing that matters, notice when your thoughts wander off. If thoughts keep popping into your mind and you have distractions around you, just keeping bringing your attention back to the inner stillness. Back to your breathing or chosen focus point. Feel at ease with whatever is going on. There are never too many distractions, just as long as you bring your awareness back, once, twice or a thousand times. It all starts with that first step.

The rest will come.

***

THE ATTITUDES OF mindfulness help us to focus our attention in a particular way and observe our thoughts and feelings without judgement.

The three aspects of mindfulness help you view your approach, so you can get the most out of your practice.

Intention – Your intention is what you hope to get from practising mindfulness.

Attention – Mindfulness is about paying attention to your inner or outer experience.

Attitude – Be present with fresh eyes in any situation without judgement.

***

REMEMBER HOW STILL the frog can be, while sitting still a frog is aware of everything going on around it but all you see from the outside is the occasional subtle rise and fall of the tummy – the breath.

The important thing is not to waste energy on what you don't have to.

A great start to all mindful practice is to stop, focus and observe – just like the frog. The frog is capable of huge jumps, but it doesn't burn out doing things it doesn't need to right now, it just focuses on this moment.

We all have the ability to be calm and sit still. Just allow yourself to stop, observing whatever is present; not changing just noticing.

If you feel frustrated sitting still like the frog just notice it – that's mindful attention. If your leg is not playing ball and keeps wriggling so you are not as still as frog, just notice it! That too is mindful attention. Once you've noticed, all you need to do is bring your attention back.

Being mindful is about paying attention in a particular way. The other most important thing is to NOTICE. Notice and you're nearly there. You can be mindful in small ways each day. By doing so, the enjoyment and pleasure of the simplest thing is transformed. Just slow it all down. Take a break, notice it. The more you practise the more you notice. Don't let the simplicities pass you by.

Decide what you read or listen to today: trust yourself and let go of the need to look at the news or the internet. Come offline for a day if it helps.

Don't worry about what others are doing, what you think you should be doing – don't judge yourself or strive to be any particular way.

Trust what you need, don't see, or speak to people who make you feel bad about yourself - you don't have to.

We oversee our emotional weather; we just need to give ourselves the right conditions to shine.

We can't ignore everything that's going on around us right now, but we can choose the way we think about it. Our emotions follow the way we think so direct them wisely.

See the sunshine in something today, move those clouds out the way.

***

Breathe ...

Have you noticed your breathing today? We breathe all day long, yet it often goes unnoticed. Try and notice some of your breaths today and see how that is for you.

Focus here and see how you can control your breathing, just by paying attention.

You can practise connecting with your breath at any time, all you have to do is notice. Meditation and yoga teach you to connect with your breath. There are many ways to connect with your breathing. Notice your breath while singing, running, walking, whenever. Really tune in and move with your breath; noticing it during these actions makes a huge difference.

We've all heard 'don't forget to breathe' at some point in our lifetime. We never 'forget' to breathe, we simply become unaware of our breathing and distance from it. We tend to hold our breath during concentration, fear, certain movement etc, but our brain always knows how to breathe.

Connecting with your breathing before sleeping really helps with better quality of sleep and can help ease anxious moments. A technique used for this is the 4-7-8 breathing method, which really relaxes your breathing. I share this with you at the end of the chapter.

Try noticing your breath a little more today and feel the benefits for you.

Your breath is your anchor.

***

Why are we never taught how to use our breath?

YOUR BREATH GUIDES you and when it is truly understood, it provides a sense of grounding felt like no other. You not only hear the spoken words but the words from the heart, too.

Of course, we all breathe each day. Our breath comes and goes, and our ears hear the sounds we tune into but, ask yourself, do you fully understand your unique breath?

Slow, deep breathing activates the 'rest and digest' response. This we could all do with more of – the opposite to 'fight-or-flight' which all too easily seems to activate instead, certainly for me!

I thought I knew how to breathe; I've been breathing all my life. Our body naturally breathes, of course, but why are we not taught when young, at school, the benefits of breathing? How to control it, how to use our breath to relax, reduce panic, be present, focus.

I for one wish this was something I was taught much earlier as the benefits are endless.

Effective breathing can help you …

- Feel less stressed.
- Promote relaxation.
- Lower your blood pressure.
- Connect with yourself.
- Ground yourself.
- Stop panic.
- Boost the immune system.
- Aid better sleep.
- Move more freely.

When practising mindfulness and meditation regularly you become aware of your breath on many occasions. When you breathe in your tummy expands. When you breathe out your tummy draws in. Tiny pauses between each breath.

When teaching mindfulness – with both children and adults – it has become clear that most people draw in their stomach when breathing in and on exhaling they push their tummy out.

When naturally breathing this won't be the case but when you are asked to bring attention sometimes people focus on the words rather than the breath itself. In becomes in. Out become out.

Do you know how to use your breath? Take a moment now to notice where you feel your own. Notice the pause between breaths, the power there. The power in the pause alone.

***

My top tips if you're feeling anxious

- Allow yourself to feel anxious, just for a moment, explore that feeling. Where do you feel it? What colour would you give it? Notice what happens when you give the anxious feelings space to just be there.

- Now try and hold on to the feeling. Naturally by holding on we learn to let go. Ever so slightly it begins to happen, trust me.

- Allow your thoughts to float away, like balloons in your hand, close your eyes and in your own time release them one by one!

- Try the letting go meditation in the Mindful Moments section (page 310) and know that these feelings will pass. The secret is to try and keep coming back to your breathing and let go as many times as you need. There is no need to rush.

My top tips if you are supporting somebody experiencing feelings of anxiety

- Best you can try not to use the phrase 'DON'T WORRY' in this situation. I know it comes from a place of love and wanting to help but essentially it's saying 'don't feel', and we can't not feel. In heightened anxiety, hearing 'don't worry' just adds extra pressure and just encourages us to suppress the emotion, which isn't healthy.

- Just open your arms and be there. It will pass.

The 4-7-8 breathing technique

DURING EXTREME PERIODS of anxiety and panic this breathing technique has been a lifesaver for me every time.

This breathing technique consists of breathing in for 4 seconds, holding for 7 seconds then breathing out for 8 seconds.

I love this technique as it really grounds me into the present moment. I started using it to help me through panic moments and particularly anxious times. It continues to be beneficial for me and I still use it today in my mindfulness practise.

It's so easy to use and very relaxing, go on, give it a try …

Close your mouth and inhale quietly through your nose

to a mental count of 4. Hold your breath for a count of 7. Exhale completely through your mouth, making a whoosh sound to a count of 8. This is one breath.

Try this when you get into bed too: repeating this technique helps lower your blood pressure to enable a more restful sleep.

⬆ Breathe in for 4 seconds.

➡ Hold for 7 seconds.

⬇ Breathe out for 8 seconds.

🔁 Repeat as many times as needed.

Remember you can explore a count that works for you. The aim is to connect with something that feels manageable, whatever that looks like, and then extend in your own time.

Audio link to 478 breathing:
https://www.room478.com/478-breathing/

Connection

Longing to find meaning, we look for something more,
Slipping into striving to reach the goals and soar.
Caught up in the rat race, life quickly passing by,
Clinging on to what feels safe, your wings were made to fly.

When looking for connection an ideal dwells in your head,
You want to fit with what seems right yet lose yourself instead.
Holding on not letting go to what has played its part,
Releasing is the key to give freedom to your heart.

Connection that has meaning sits within the unknown,
It creeps up out of nowhere and often leaves you thrown,
Once more you begin to question, your mind doesn't feel it's right,
You shut it down for safety and push it out of sight.

Again, veiled in the safety net of fitting in once more,
Life goes on and so do you, but you know what's behind the door.
What's meant for you won't pass you by if you're brave enough to feel,
Lean into your knowing, to what you hear; for that is real.

Be kind to where you've come from, grateful for it all,
No longer shut down who you are; climb over every wall.

Connection to true meaning, be freely who you are,
Follow every dream you have, and you will carry far.
Being present with each single breath, opens up this voice,
A time will come when you see so clear, you no longer have a choice.

***

Chapter 6

Connection

IT HIT ME: somewhere along the line I'd completely lost myself. Where did this happen? I felt as though I'd been thumped in the chest. A heavy feeling took over as I sat at the table of unfamiliar faces in front of me.

I froze for a while; the space open for me to enquire within. My feelings began to rise and this time I didn't shut them down. I could feel a strength, a deep sense of knowing that I needed to be with what I felt. There was no need to fit into a box or say the right thing this time – and this wouldn't be the last time I felt this way either. My hand felt sweaty as I picked up my pen and started to write freely what was present.

As I sat amongst those strangers, it was time to reflect and share (if we wanted) following the meditation. Listening to others speak freely, I started to ease, the internal shift ever so slightly rose. I was able to be with what came up. It was my turn. The words just spilled out of my mouth, 'When exactly was it that I completely lost myself?' What had sat deep inside me for so long ever so slightly became unstuck, particles freeing and rising to the surface like bubbles in a glass of lemonade.

What a question. I realised that I had gradually faded away, sunk beneath so many layers. Disconnected. To get to the route of this huge question I had presented myself with, I knew I would have to address all the places where I had forgotten who I was, and this was going to get uncomfortable. Before I knew it the tears fell, streaming down my face. In some ways it was a release, a comfort: to say it aloud, to feel the echo of my own voice. I'd been wearing this mask for a long time.

I had just taken part in a cacao ceremony. For those of you who don't know, cacao comes from the edible seed of the cacao tree (the same tree used to make chocolate) in its raw state, after it's been left to dry in the sun and ferment. In a cacao ceremony the sharing of cacao and drinking this together aids the opening of our hearts. I can confirm I was laden with an open heart, which I do seem to carry at the best of times, but this felt different. It was a new feeling: I had compassion for myself which felt quite alien before now.

One of the ladies at the table walked over and put her arms around me. I leaned in and felt comfort receiving support from someone who was essentially a stranger – yet at the same time I felt safer to be vulnerable and open in this space than with people I'd known for years. I felt connected and I was able to be just as I was, no hiding.

Connection took on a whole new significance and I began to see that when I connected to my soul, my purpose, I was free to be me, who I really am under the layers. I had lost myself, become caught up in what connection 'should' look like, silenced that whisper from within. Finally, I felt present enough to elevate that voice.

Whilst researching for greater understanding of my own detachment I read the following quote, shared by Marisa Peer: 'Find connection – avoid rejection!'

Isn't this something we all want? To find connection so that we aren't rejected? After my breakdown and breakthrough, I kept thinking about this and exploring where exactly the disconnection came from. Looking back, I see now that it was largely in fear of being rejected and how it relates to so many aspects of life.

Nobody likes feeling rejected. Consequently, at times we become desperate to find a connection to fit in or please in any way that we can. The desperate search for this connection can take us away from ourselves and can create patterns that aren't healthy, becoming never-ending if we allow it.

Have you ever done any of the following? Worn clothes you felt uncomfortable in. Pretended to know something to go along with conversation. Said you've watched a movie or read a book that you haven't. Not spoken your true beliefs in front of others for fear of not fitting in. Not ordered a meal you've really wanted. There are endless examples of this if we explore.

Why do we do this? Doing, saying, wearing things we don't align with. Feeling like we just want to fit in. Desperate to find a connection with something or someone so that we blend into space just to feel some sense of being. Scared to face rejection from the conversation or the crowd. Scared to be you. It's no wonder we start to slip away from ourselves ever so slightly until one day you feel lost from who you once were.

When finding connection within ourselves, not rejecting parts of us, instead connecting with all that makes us unique and beautiful, strength resurfaces. This way we experience true, authentic connection with something that really matters: the one thing that will always be with us.

I am always learning but as I continue my search, the more it makes sense. The fear of being rejected is present through all walks of life. It can be so strong that the desire to connect in any way we can is often to the detriment to who we are or how we want to be. Rather than spend endless time trying to avoid rejection we need to lean into who we are, releasing the need to fit in. In turn, those true connections are established.

Can you connect with yourself instead of losing yourself for fear of being rejected?

I thought on these lessons, the reflections risen when asking myself these questions. I'd now come to realise I was scared of rejection, but why? Weeks went by, and I found I was pulled back to this reality of hiding who I was once more. I had tried so hard to fit in so I didn't feel rejection, projecting into the future so often that I was never truly present to see what had slowly been creeping up. The anxiety constantly felt like a huge mask and yet it remained my tried and tested coping mechanism to carry me through each day. I had been resisting the real difficulties for a long time. The fear of being left, disconnected.

On that particular day, my energy was so low that everything felt flat, including the way I felt loved by others. The disconnect ever-present and all the while I was slipping further and further away from myself. I knew I was changing inside; the more connected I felt to myself the less I hid, yet with this I began to see that the distance grew. Things changed around me, people I once saw all the time, now less frequently, and my time was spent differently, too. My time now in ceremony, welcoming the cacao and raw emotion instead of the wine and morning anxiety. By not fitting in I allowed myself to drift. Feeling whole and gravitating to space where feeling this way was normal. Dancing ecstatically, no inhibitions yet connected to the energy of the people around me. The music fully inside my body, the beat moving my energy flow intuitively, freely ... it felt great. If you haven't tried it, I highly recommend it. Sober raves are the way forward.

I see that all the years I spent intoxicated I was longing to feel connected, I was blocking something out, pushing down emotion. But now doing the work, healing, allowing it all to rise, the connections naturally came and the spaces to feel that same buzz (but so much better for me!) keep coming, even now.

It comes back to love, the feeling of love. The feeling deep inside sits in the beauty of connected spaces like this. Eighty per cent of the time, all those boozy nights out I wanted the same result: connection, movement and love, yet the night often ended messy: tears flowing and a really sore head the next day.

It's taken me a while now to unravel the changes, with wounds surfacing but finally a new love present: the love I have for me, just as I am. Never mind what anyone else thinks. Of course, it hasn't been easy finding my way back here.

How do we find our way back? Not back to a time when you once felt a certain way, but how do we get in touch with who we truly are, discovering those all-important things that you really find connection with? We all have *ikigai*, 'a reason to live'. In Japanese, 'ik' means 'life' and 'gai' describes value or worth. Your *ikigai* is your life purpose or your bliss. It's what brings you joy and inspires you to get out of bed every day. When you align with your *ikigai* you sit in a state of happiness, your reason for being, your bliss. It's in these moments that life is really quite something and it feels as though time speeds up and goes by so quickly. (*Ikigai: The Japanese Secret to a Long and Happy Life* is a brilliant book on just this if you haven't yet read it.)

I feel I'm taking a very long path to find my way back to myself and at times I take constant diversions. The urge to find meaning, find connections with myself and others, trying to keep up and fit in, all the while striving for more.

I notice that I hold on far longer than necessary to that which makes me feel safe, in my comfort zone. You may find you slip into a well engrained habit because you essentially know the outcome, it's safer that way, or is it? Sticking to what we know keeps us safely in the comfort zone and yet even the comfort zone can eventually be feared. Burrowing yourself further into this comfort zone makes it much harder to step into the powerful place of growth. But the lessons will keep being thrown at you until you pause, stop and listen.

***

IT'S CHALLENGING – heartbreaking in fact – when something that once was your everything becomes an unrecognisable vision. Distance presents as you slip away from what you know, but so much more is available if we're brave enough to listen to our intuition, tune into what we feel and find connection with this voice. The more we listen, the more guidance we receive.

So often we think we haven't got time, we tell others we haven't time either. Yet if it really matters the time will be available to you. We can't have time for it all but when you start to prioritise what makes you feel connected the time presents itself. The things you really want to make time for, you will! The people you really want to see, you'll reach out to and make time to see them. The events that are really important, you'll be there for. We feel connected when we can be fully ourselves, whatever this looks like. The more time we spend doing this the easier it is to find connection, not only with others but also ourselves.

I went to another festival recently and I went alone. It was so freeing; I could just attend the classes I wanted to and go in my own time. At the festival I met so many people, all singing the same song. Connection so important yet the deepest connection often felt when sharing space with people I'd only known for five minutes. The realisation for us all coming to the surface that those times once spent moaning about others, being concerned with what others did last night, all pulls you further away from what we all long: to be connected. Now I often feel most connected when alone.

Anxiety can take us down a rabbit hole, pressure to fit in, do more, say yes. However, the depth of your own connection, your understanding of self, brings strength to connect with what you choose to say yes to; those decisions coming from a place that suits you, not simply pleasing everyone else.

***

I SHARED A quote with a friend of mine recently.

You're going to hit a point where you're no longer interested in convincing people that how you feel and who you are is valid and decide that as long as you know your truth and what works for you, that's all that matters. – **Tiny Buddha**

A time will come where you begin to see that what you need is important, and space highlights that you do need to put yourself first. Start living for you and in turn the path seems to unfold more naturally.

***

I READ A while ago that 'spirit' comes from the Latin word for 'breath', and like breath, spirit is considered a fundamental part of being alive. We also use spirit to mean 'the general mood or intent': 'She's in good spirits today … great team spirit … that's the spirit.'

You may feel someone's spirit. Acknowledge someone appearing in good spirits but have you felt your own spirit?

Are you in touch with your life force, your energy, your will? Is spirit the connection? Is spirit love?

Allow yourself a moment to explore these questions if you feel drawn to them.

***

IN THE DEEPEST sense, the breath itself is the ultimate gift of spirit. I now understand this as when I connect with my breath, I connect with my energy. When I'm not in my thoughts, when I'm feeling instead, I'm connecting with myself. I couldn't understand this at first as I was always in my thoughts when feeling anxious.

I thought of spirit in terms of where you feel a spiritual connection with external things – something, somewhere or someone – I know it can be this too, but the more I learn about it, I realise it's much deeper than this. I now feel spirit is the answer within us, the answer we often search so long for; our spirit lies in our heart, I like to think. So when you stop to connect with your heart, you will find your spirit and fully connect, you will be guided back to yourself, to love. It's the pot of gold at the end of the rainbow. It's all parts of your being coming together. Your breath, your anchor; mindfully coming back to the connection within. Mediation threading it all together. When you find the connection with yourself, you find your spirit. Your spirit connects all of you together. The willingness to be all you are. Connected.

***

WE CAN FIND a deeper connection to ourselves by spending more time in nature. Nature constantly shows us how things always change, but can still flourish.

When feeling down or anxious the thought of doing anything at all can sometimes feel too much. If you can, taking yourself outside even for a short while can really transform your mood and in turn your whole day.

Spending just twenty minutes outside amongst greenery, in nature, can be as beneficial as antidepressants. Nature is a natural stimulus which helps regulate our nervous system. Even looking at nature has positive effects. So many beautiful seasonal sights to help lift your mood. Nature: our natural antidepressant.

Time and time again, I feel the call to walk in the woods, to get grounded, feel connected and breathe. Feel the energy.

Try surrounding yourself in green – colour, energy, crystals, nature – and see how you feel. The effects are quite remarkable.

We also appear to ruminate less in nature. Helping us be present and not dwell or overthink too much, which helps reduce depression and anxiety.

If things seem a bit much right now, take a little time outside if you can.

***

Nurture too an important part of self-care. Think about what lights you up. Spend some time breathing, being present and see what comes to mind..

When we begin to connect with ourselves time alone is no longer felt as loneliness.

Solitude – this isn't loneliness.

There is a lot to be said for putting your own needs first and implementing that element of self-care, I admire it. Recognising your own needs is important, but, unfortunately, some people are just inherently selfish! Those people don't care about how they act, whereas self-care takes place when time out is needed, but with plenty of communication about this need. This is also the difference when maintaining a healthy connection. Connection is felt when communication is strong, when truths are spoken and deep listening evoked. We can't expect people to constantly show up for us: things change, circumstances change, and we move forward. What once filled much of your time may no longer be present at all and this is ok.

***

Taking time for yourself is needed, it's a must! I used to think this act of looking after myself was selfish. I felt bad for taking time out and saying no to others. Squeezing in as much as I possibly could until I was burnt out. I now understand establishing and maintaining self-care is vital.

Have you ever felt this way?

A reminder to us all:

'Put your own oxygen mask on first!'
'You can't pour from an empty cup.'

Both of these are true: we must fill ourselves up, so we are full. Overflowing in fact. The quality of what you can then give and share with others is far more beneficial for you and those around you. By giving yourself time to regenerate, every part of you can function better.

So if like me, you currently feel putting yourself first makes you self-centred if you, please don't – it is not selfish. It's ok to take some time for you, as much as you need in fact.

Take time, before you have to make time.

***

I regularly practised yoga and used the word 'namaste' before I understood its meaning fully.

Only in later years when practising meditation and reading different books did I discover its meaning, so here I share with you what I read, so I can pass on the knowledge.

Namaste represents the idea that all are one. That despite what you see on the outside, it affirms we are all made of the same stuff inside.

If the spiritual traditions of yoga could be encapsulated in one word, it might be namaste. This Sanskrit word brings about the essence of oneness, and an understanding of the true nature of reality.

One of the most common translations of namaste is 'The divine light in me bows to the divine light within you.'

However, there are many other beautiful meanings and translations of namaste, such as:

I honour the place in you where the entire universe dwells.
I bow to the place in you that is love, light and joy.
When you and I bow to our true nature, we are one.
My soul recognises your soul.
We are the same, we are one.
I honour the place in you that is the same as it is in me.

This one word opening the path of connection. When looking for connection it is important that we recognise what already resides in ourselves too.

***

I have found such deep connection through music: it evokes memories, joy, pain, all sorts of emotion. The song plays out and I have space to be fully with it. Music is so powerful; the effects are unbelievable. Recently music has helped me resurface memories and make peace with them. It has also taken my meditation on a different route which has been enjoyable.

As music can absorb our attention, it acts as a distraction while helping us explore emotions at the same time. Making music a great aid to meditation, preventing the mind from wandering.

Listening to music can have a tremendously relaxing effect on our minds and bodies. Music, in short, can act as a powerful stress management tool in our lives. It's even been proven to evoke memories for those living with Alzheimer's.

We are so lucky to be able to access music so freely and in return it can free us. Try exploring some different music and see how you feel connected to it. Which memories surface? Notice how it reconnects you with a moment in time, those feelings that were once long forgotten, now felt once more, thoughts now again present. Explore resistance, joy, love, tears, and notice what is present for you.

***

Find yourself!

One of the most powerful things you can find, is you!

For some this is later in life, for others this may never fully come. To live a life through what's expected can be draining.

I heard this quote again recently: 'Youth is wasted on the young'. When reflecting in my journal I thought about this, my youth. Mine was spent with much time wasting thoughts on what others think, what I should wear, have I said the right thing. Trying to please and fit in, not being true to me. The thing is – what are we trying to fit into? Who is authentically living their truth? I now see I wasted much time and energy worrying.

When young and leaving school, there is so much energy to be burnt and so many choices laid in front of you, yet the freedom and understanding to enjoy it can be clouded by the judgements and pressures of how and what you should be.

I wouldn't change my past and choices, they have brought me to today, but looking back has been an interesting reflection. With wisdom and maturity, being free to be who I am, I see how that energy could have been channelled in many other ways.

How wonderful it would be if every child was able to find themselves early on and be at peace in the moment without all this added pressure and judgement, youth lived freely, authenticity, truthfully – being who they are. Emotions welcomed, and instead of pushing everything down, space open for them all to be felt and in turn processed. This should be part of everyday schooling: incorporating mindfulness and meditation, positive affirmation, gratitude. What a huge benefit to replace the learnt behaviours of do more, do better, be more. What happened to be you, you are enough, who are you?

Quite often the journey to self begins when you hit rock bottom: you face a wall and can go no further. Depression or anxiety may play a part and you know you can't move forward in this way any more. You then find … you.

I am so grateful for reaching my wall, bringing me on this rollercoaster ride to connect with who I am. It's so important to find who you truly are, to connect with yourself, releasing the judgement. To know and enjoy you; not living through someone else or for someone else.

Of course, we want to love and feel loved, but we can only have the most heart-warming of relationships with others once we know who we are.

***

How to find yourself

NOTICING YOUR BREATH is one of the easiest ways to bring your awareness to the present moment.

Take a moment to focus on your breath: bring your attention to where you feel your breath in your body. Each time your mind wanders, wherever your thoughts take you, just gently bring it back to the breath.

The aim here is to take eight purposeful deep breaths. Or

as many or as little as you feel comfortable with.

Breathe deeply, and on each inhale, focus on where you feel this in your body. Slowly release and exhale. Repeat eight times.

Do you feel better?

If you feel overwhelmed, notice this feeling and return to your breath when you remember.

***

CONNECTION IS SOMETHING we all want, but connections we thought may be there forever can slip away. We all change as we grow and through this the people and places that surround us change too. I believe the ones that meant to stay will do and those who leave us have brought into our lives what we were meant to experience and learn together. This doesn't make it any less difficult when a connection that once felt so strong just slips away and is unrecognisable as it once was.

Silence speaks a thousand words and when you are chasing and reaching for this deep connection it's hard to see those gaps. Yet when we pause, when we stop and see what's left, the silence often speaks for itself.

Sorry is a word that we all say time and time again, I used to use it a lot; the moment anyone pulled me up on anything I found myself apologising for myself, my tears, my emotions, my ideas, my opinions. It goes on. Also, on the receiving end of sorry, much of the time it falls into a dead space, the constant sorry for lack of time, connection. Yet if you really want something you make it work. The deeper the connection with yourself, the stronger your inner strength becomes, elevating your intuition and conviction, allowing you to begin to see what's real and what's not.

***

I love Dino Hira's analogy about flowers only blooming when there is an environment filled with sun, water, and love. If a flower struggles to bloom, perhaps it's because one of these elements is missing. Flowers and plants need space too, don't they? We can learn a lot from them. If the flower isn't blooming, we fix the environment not the flower itself.

Reading this really struck a chord within, it's such an important reminder of just how amazing each and every one of us is, in our own way. We don't need fixing or changing: we just need the right environment. One that allows us to be open, to be whole.

How many times have you tried to change yourself, instead of the external factors around you? We don't need to change in order to fix ourselves or fit into somebody else's ideal, or what works for them. We need to be able to be our true self and be content with this.

So next time things don't feel right for you, don't think you need to change yourself. Have a look around you at your environment, the company you keep, the life you are living and ask yourself what needs to change there.

Don't take away your existing beauty or feel the need to change to fit in. Be true to yourself, connect with your true meaning, your purpose and be freely who you are. Fit into you. Make space for people who can enhance this journey.

Now you've found you, you'll find your people, the true connections will come, as will a time when you see so clearly, that you no longer have a choice to be anything less than you.

***

The Heart's Path

As you allow your heart to open, you begin to clearly see,
At times this can feel scary when you don't know what's to be.
Now exposing up this gateway to what's truly deep inside,
It's vulnerable, the unknown, with no mask to hide behind.

The alternative – to keep the doors closed to all you truly are,
The dreams, the truth, the love you crave then seen only from afar.
Allow your heart to open, connect to what's within,
Your purpose and your passion, it no longer wants to dim.

Permit your light to shine from deep down in your heart,
You came here to be all of you, each and every part.
Don't run from your desire, lean in with every breath,
Dive into each experience before there's nothing left.
Taking steps to do the right thing every day,

Pleasing others, avoiding risks: do you want to walk
that way?
Your heart it knows the answer, it guides you right
each time,
You hear the voice then shut it down, frightened
to let it shine.

Your mind speaks up, your ears tune in, it alludes
you once again,
An alternative, a safer route; you think that it's your
friend.
Moments pass and days go by, the mind it paves
a path,
One you could walk so differently if you listened
to your heart.

Stop and take a moment, connect back to your
breath,
Let the voice inside your heart dare to take its depth.
The magic and the wonder, adventure lies ahead,
Just stop to take a moment, connect and put the
mind to bed.
The heart beats strong, the message clear of what
you want to do,
Lose your mind a little bit, love will carry through.
Smile when you listen to what you have to say,
Your dreams become reality, love now paves the way.

If you are brave enough to walk on the path your
heart speaks,
The mind it starts adjusting and making little tweaks.
Catching up along the way, it understands now too,

By taking rest with each deep breath, it sees it now;
sees you!

The bravery, the darker days, those moments not
fitting in,
The message now lands perfectly, when being you,
you win.
Those times spent an imposter, embarrassed by the
tears,
The mind now caught up with the heart and sees
they washed away the fears.

If you dare to show emotion you connect with
something more,
The journey you were destined for, the heart wants
you to soar.
Breathing in this lifetime, wide open, being all that
you are,
Listen to your heartbeat, this path will take you far.

Free and feeling love each and every day,
Even on those darker days, your heart, it knows
the way.
Inside lie all the answers, the key to all the joy,
Walk on this path, welcome it all; there's no need
to destroy.

Your memories, your sadness, and any lived through
pain,
Acceptance is the first step; from history we gain.
Stay true to what you hear inside,
Walking on the heart's path, there's no need to hide.

You didn't come here to be anything less than you,
So, listen to what you know is right, you know what
you must do.

Listen to that message that comes from in your
heart, your feet grounded on the floor,
Knock down all the barriers and walk through
every door.

***

Chapter 7

The Heart's Path

WE FALL IN and out of love many times in our lifetime. This love will never look the same as the last: we grow, we change, and the love we are so desperate for changes, too. The more you connect to yourself and listen to your heart, the way you give and receive love changes. This is what I have noticed. Through my own experience and after talking to many about love during writing this book, I believe we are all at some point so desperate for love. That feeling, longing to be complete, the attachment to another to fill this void, to be enough, validated.

When pursuing this love, we seem willing to not only change ourselves but also sacrifice what is truly desired, too. Scared to listen deeply to what you know your heart wants and needs, so, for a period you settle for less. At times we also miss so many of the beautiful moments of love in front of our eyes. That person who drives you insane may be in their own way showing love a multitude of times but because it's not the way you like to feel loved, it is missed. The more in tune we can get to what lights us up and makes us feel whole, the more of this love we feel.

It can be the hardest thing, to follow your heart, especially when it's not able to grab hold of what it wants, love flowing out but not coming back in. Girl likes boy, boy likes another girl. Girl gets boy, girl's heart stamped on from a great height. Protection comes into place and girl loses herself to impress boy. Girl takes years to find her way back to her true self, finds boy, boy can't spend time with girl. Girl once more stood alone. Full circle! Many variations of this occur and boys can be heartbroken too! The thing we all have in common is the love we can give to ourselves.

The ultimate love is in your heart, inside you and when you connect back to this place, no attachment to anything outside of this, remember it is felt right there; the ultimate place to feel connected.

***

Again, bolted awake! Its 4.44am and this hits hard. I know where I lost myself and it wasn't in just one moment, a single moment in my lifetime where I disappeared; it was a series of events and it was happening time and time again. Over and over.

I keep losing myself under this desperation to be loved, loved in the exact way that I give love. Ignoring the messages from my heart each time. If I didn't feel loved back, I lost who I was again, trying to be perfect in somebody's eyes. People-pleasing and burning myself out showing others just how I felt.

Where do I keep going wrong?

Why am I not loveable? I just want to be somebody's first choice.

This has been a bumpy road; I feel like I'm running. Through the woods and just out of sight somebody is shooting arrows at me, they tear my clothes as they come so close but don't quite catch my skin and I keep running.

I'm in a lot of pain. Healing is hard, it's painful. Am I brave enough? I've wanted to give up so many times. Feeling unheard again and again. Do I stop running and take the arrowhead on, full force? It feels as though I have.

***

WHEN YOU PAUSE, you can listen, you hear the messages clear as day from deep inside. I tried to be someone else and wanted to be liked always, but a hard realisation; not everyone is going to like you and that's ok. What works one day may not work the next. Learning step by step to be with what is, to be present and come back again and again.

When working through my own struggles, I've had to step away from many people. I've had to say no to a lot of things, you could say letting people down. But to freely feel my emotion, to be open with what matters and connect to who I am, knowing not everyone will fit and realising this is fine. If you feel something, allow yourself to feel it, spend more time in spaces where it's safe to show up just as you are.

***

Letting go is difficult, but it's necessary, I feared being lonely so often I clung on, or went out when I may not have wanted to, all so I didn't have to sit with how I felt. Avoidance played a big part in my coping mechanisms. It took me off track many a time.

Does loneliness have to mean you are physically on your own, nobody to see or speak to? Or can you be surrounded by people, work, events, seeming to have it all together and still feel that isolation inside?

It's easy for me to conclude that both are possible and something I have felt.

From time to time things aren't the way we want them to be, and coping looks different for us all. Harbouring that sense of loss carries pain, sadness, an unsettled feeling. What are we to do to move through it?

Prior to practising mindfulness and meditation, whenever I felt lost, anxious or had a problem of any kind I would hide behind never-ending lists of things to do. My way through looked a little like: digging a hole, burying the problem, running past it again and again at high speed, stamping it down a little further, thinking it would go away. Suppressing the emotions, yet all the while the feelings present, just not shown.

Had I resolved anything? Did I feel better? Had the loneliness passed? No! I had just accumulated more pressure, piled on by myself – in turn allowing no space to process how I felt.

Living in my thoughts left little space. Crushing connection along the way and creating those lonely pockets inside.

It can be a huge challenge to face how we feel and think about what we truly want; a tough road may lie ahead. Allow the emotion to rise, by taking that initial step and simply bringing awareness to your thoughts and feelings, it can help you move through.

***

ASK YOURSELF THE following questions:

- Are you on the path your heart desires?
- Do you regularly settle for less so that you don't let others down?
- Do you notice the wonderful things you do have but sometimes they are clouded with lack?
- Are you happy on your own? (Remember, that love we connect with shouldn't rely on anything external.)
- Are you holding on to something that is just time to let go of?

Asking ourselves regular questions like these enables us to connect deeper with the true calling of your heart. Spend a little time exploring this and see what rises for you. There isn't a right way to do so. I like to sit in meditation (pen and paper at the ready) and ask questions, connect with my heart, and simply wait and see what comes to me, then I freely write what is present. Personally, I have gained a lot of insight through this process and see that I block what I often already know. But seeing it written down in front of me helps connect back to my heart. It starts by finding a place where it's safe to be vulnerable, to share how I feel, if it feels right. To be free with this emotion.

***

Happiness is something everybody wants to feel. We buy 'stuff' to fill that void of always searching, needing, wanting – more, more, more! Yet we all have it already, we are born with it, and we create it.

Have a look around you.

Alter your perspective and really see what's in front of you.

Persevere with your dreams.

Patiently see all the places already filled with happiness.

Inside yourself happiness can be found.

Now is where you are, what do you see?

Encourage yourself as you would others.

See what you have already, what makes you feel complete.

Search within yourself for deeper meaning, it's not in material things.

HAPPINESS – The way to live your life. Not something to search for.

**

TAKE A MOMENT now and think about or write down what makes you happy.

Where do you find those moments where time goes by so fast, and you are present?
Where do you feel fully connected? Alive and free?
Where do you lose track of time completely? You look at your watch and the time has flown by.
Where are the pockets already in your life where you feel there is no need to change?

Just taking a moment now to reflect on what's come up for you.

New day – start today!

DO YOU FIND you sometimes put things off? I know I do. I did the same thing when writing this book.

Do you wait until you have more time, you're not as busy, not as tired? The weather's right, you have more money etc. It has been said many times before, that we will always want more, whatever that may be for us individually: a promotion at work, a pay rise, a holiday, peace and quiet, some time out. More money, more sleep, more chocolate. This is of course quite generalised but most of the time it's too easy to get caught in the cycle of always needing just a bit more. Then once we've got that one more thing, we then need something else.

When is it ever enough or ever the right time?

Putting things off until the right moment, the next week, this could keep happening forever. There will never be the perfect time. The only time is now, and you already have what you need to get started: you! This applies to all the wonderful things you are fully capable of achieving, the things you want to begin. The time to start is today. However small a step towards what you want. Make it happen, it's a brand-new week, a new day for you to fill.

Make something in your day about what you want, something you enjoy. Something you'd like to make happen.

You can start today, even if it's the smallest step, we all must begin somewhere. Even if it's a thought you don't dismiss this time; a note of what you are going to do next; a little research. You just need to take the first step, and some days this step means resting!

***

Everyone is a genius. But if you judge a fish by its ability to climb a tree, it will live its whole life believing that it is stupid. – **Albert Einstein**

This has got to be one of my favourite ever quotes. We often measure ourselves against others, making us doubt our own abilities. These negative patterns are unhelpful, it's ok to realise we are not good at everything or even the same things. Just like the fish: it doesn't want to be judged on climbing a tree but swimming the ocean.

We are pushed at school, at work, always needing to strive

for more or better (as noted in the attitudes of mindfulness, see non-striving on page 55). One person's strength may be somebody else's weakness, but it doesn't make one better than the other. If you are a highly skilled musician, you don't need to be judged by a maths test. Equally, if you want to be an accountant your ability to play the saxophone won't matter in this instance either. This doesn't mean we shouldn't do or try things we may not excel in but just realise it doesn't define us or take away from the amazing qualities you already have if you don't get it all right.

Just because you can't do something, it doesn't make you stupid. Our abilities are different: if you waste your time focusing on what others may be doing better than you or constantly comparing yourself, your own genius will be hidden, could sit undiscovered or even pass you by.

Instead, do what you enjoy and strive for what you love and you will thrive in that environment. It's ok to walk different paths. Find what you love and make mistakes along the way. It's ok to let go of the things you no longer want, the things that are not good for you. Make space for who and what matters to you.

Believe in yourself.

***

Three things cannot be long hidden: the sun, the moon, and the truth. – **The Buddha**

WE KNOW THAT certain things are always there, even if we

don't see them, such as the sun and moon. They may hide but they always come out again.

Truth in all walks of life and relationships has significant importance. The truth sets us free to live an honest life and enables us to give and receive love fully. Just like the sun and moon, the truth can be hidden for a time, but it always comes out in the end. Be it pain, change, or a new path.

This applies to our own truths, too. You can try and hide behind all sorts of different things or covers throughout life, not fully being true to who you are but your truths will show eventually. The sooner you allow this, you will live a happier life. You will be set free by living your truths.

In the Zen tradition, they sometimes describe the mind like a glass of cloudy water. The advice given is: if you want to clarify the water, you must stop shaking, stirring and fussing.

Just like this tradition, the truth will always become clear, clarified just like the water. Once all the busyness, fussing and extreme behaviours are out the way, the truth sits, waiting patiently, always present behind whatever it's hidden.

Truth is the actual meaning of something: we may not always like the truth, but we need truth to have honest relationships. We can only start seeing things clearly – including ourselves – once we start being honest with ourselves.

When I finally stopped, I saw beyond it all, the truth. I just wanted to be loved and that's why I kept searching.

This truth is particularly hard when it means letting go, releasing people from your life who have taken up space in some way, but you know aren't doing you any good. Even when you feel love so deeply for that person, knowing that you must let go is hard, but the truth is, you know. Deep down you feel it, desperate to come first, be that first and last thought of the day but it slips away, and it hurts until you start acting on that resolution to find a different kind of love.

***

Most people will talk the talk; few will walk the walk.
– Maria W. Stewart

WHICH ONE WOULD you rather be?

It can be easy to hide behind a screen, a mask, pretending to be something we're not. Entertaining the idea of something more appealing, but actually taking action never surfaces. I've been asking myself this question of late: would I rather talk the talk, or finally walk the walk? Part of showing up each day is to try and stay true to who I am, to what means something to me. Doing this has led me back towards what lights me up, to becoming fully me, walking my walk the best I can each day. It's not always easy and sometimes it can feel lonely, but it's necessary.

Through life we are all guilty of saying bad things, swept up in conversations we go along with that aren't always our own true beliefs. We take on things and do things, but do we like that behaviour or is it all for show?

Journeying to find yourself enables you to truly walk your walk, practise and believe the things you speak of as important. Now I feel I embody my truth the best I can, but previously I was guilty of talking the talk and not walking the walk. I'm sure we all know someone or have been guilty in some aspect of not sticking to our beliefs. As you grow and find yourself, some people or things may not fit any more: this is ok. Holding on to thoughts, feelings or even people who don't align with you any more isn't necessary. The right ones will stay.

Live a life that's true to you, that sits right with you, and you will discover all the happiness right here. This very book is part of showing up for me. Don't be afraid to walk the path that feels true to you. Take off the mask and remember to smile when you do.

***

LOVE IS HARD. It's honest, it opens raw emotion, evoking healing and wonder alike. It can hit you so hard and then break you more than you ever thought possible, and yet how often do we go back for more? The heart holds strong throughout and, despite the highs and lows, it keeps beating.

When you're told you're loved it's an instant uplift, a dopamine hit and you want more. But when that love doesn't feel the same as when you give it, once more it breaks you. Round and round we go. So how do you connect to the path your heart wants you to take? What if you know where to go but can't get there? What if you're deeply in love but the timing doesn't work? What if you give all the love you can and it's never enough? What if you know things should be different but you cling on anyway? There are so many complications to love, but ultimately, despite it all, love is what it comes back to. When you start to listen to the messages felt in your heart, you start to see yourself, to love yourself and from here the strength is found. When you attach love to something or someone you will feel a range of emotions, this love can be beautiful, yet also complicated, with many lessons attached. When you love you, all of you, the love you receive and draw in feels different, the lessons are easier to move through and you see that you will always be there.

Truth

ULTIMATELY, LIVING TRUTHFULLY, speaking truthfully, remaining true to who you are enables you to live your life with no regrets, no worries – nothing hanging over you.

To hear the truth you must listen, forgive and let go of who or what isn't good for you. Sometimes people simply expect too much from you and you may not have the ability to give much back; it doesn't mean they are bad people, but neither are you if you are simply being true to yourself, taking what you need and not pushing yourself to limits to please others. Being in an environment with people who don't see or recognise your true self doesn't enable you to live truthfully either, it's difficult. Sometimes we need to walk away or take a pause from people or situations that are no longer good for us, knowing letting go is far healthier … as hard as this truth may be.

Ask yourself: twenty years, fifty years from now, would you rather regret doing the thing? Or regret *not* doing the thing?

We hurt ourselves the most when not telling the truth. If you lie about something it hangs over you and removes the ability to live freely. This will apply to anyone who lies to you too. If you don't listen to what you want or need, are you being truthful to yourself? We need to find middle ground and be honest with ourselves and others.

It's so beneficial to our growth to really create the space to listen to ourselves and those around us. Once we do the truth comes to the surface. This may not always be easy to do but to enable freedom you need to accept all of you, even things you may not be proud of or have difficulty accepting. We all live with pressures, the natural response of feeling bad, wanting to fit in, to please others, constant expectations from social media, the news and influence all around us, but you must tell the truth to be free. It's all too easy to roll along to fit in, but is that who you even are or want to be? The truth: it's you who needs to hear it.

***

IF IT FEELS right, journal on these questions, allow these questions to enter your heart.

- What do you love about you?
- What is it that makes your heart feel full?
- Who are you with or what are you doing when time goes by so quickly? Your *ikigai*!
- When are you in your flow state?

- What do you enjoy doing?
- Who are you when you accept every step you've taken?
- How does it feel to know that you are enough just as you are?

Remember, it's often the things you *didn't* do that you look back and wish you had.

The power of NO

HAVE YOU EVER felt the power of saying no? Say no so you can get what you need, help you do what you feel is right, connect to who you are.

- Why are we afraid to say no?
- Why is saying no seen as negative much of the time?
- Have you ever gone along with something that you really wanted to say no to?
- Been out somewhere you didn't want to go? Taken part in something? Said something?
- Why do we not say no? What are we scared of?

Saying no is just as acceptable as saying yes. Contrarily, sometimes saying yes can have a negative impact and saying no may give you a positive result.

Ask yourself: What do I want? Does this feel right? 'Yes' doesn't mean the right way or the right answer; it's ok to question things and not feel obliged.

If you can't do it today, then don't! By saying no, you are actually often saying yes to something that you need.

If it doesn't feel right – don't do it!

If it doesn't make you feel good, you can say no!

Saying no really has as many benefits as saying yes!

***

EACH AND EVERY day things are asked of us: the pressures we put on ourselves, the constant tasks at the ready if we let them. It's all too easy to get sucked into one more email, a phone call, a bit of extra work, just one more favour, your job etc. – this list could go on for some time and if you let it, it can take over until there is no time left for you. I fell into this trap for a very long time – for years in fact. Things soon become expected in all walks of life by us, by others: this is all too normal, and I'm sure we've all experienced it. The thing is, we have the power to say no; we don't have to do all of it. There comes a point where you have to say no, to pause, to take a breath, find some space and once more connect to who you are.

All too soon, we're simply expected to do certain things, they become habit. So to start saying no to something we've always done almost feels rude.

However, once I realised I can say no, that it's my choice, I've seen more things get noticed: you stand out when you say no. Your opinion matters. What you need matters. If you just say yes all the time, you end up falling in line with the default position, things get taken for granted, they can go unseen.

We need to say no at times to develop healthy relationships and to fulfil what we believe in. We also need to respect when others say no.

Toddlers say no without a bad feeling in sight, but they remain loved and listened to. This needn't go away as we get older, we just allow it to by thinking we must follow suit and do as we 'should.'

I'm not saying walk around saying no all the time, we won't want to always say no of course. But it's important to remember that saying no is not bad; it's healthy to say no when you need to and it's ok.

Don't feel obliged: if it's not right for you or you can't cope with it today – say no!

***

Intimacy

INTO-ME-SEE. I HEARD this on a Jeff Warren meditation and listened to it about three times. I had to start writing my thoughts as I explored this; it really woke something up inside of me.

The word intimacy: closeness between people in personal relationships. It's what builds over time as you connect with someone, grow to care about each other, and feel more and more comfortable during your time together. It can include physical or emotional closeness, or even a mix of the two.

Do you ever have times when you don't feel as close to someone as you once were? That the intimacy, the emotional connection drops out. After hearing this one phrase and journaling on it, a lot fell into place for me. I started to explore many of my own relationships. To see into someone, you get them, you see who they really are. Likewise, if you change and the people closest to you don't then see into you, they don't see this person and as a result the connection isn't the same. It's lost; perhaps temporarily until they can see into the new parts of you and connect with this.

If you can't see in, you can't fully connect. Sometimes connections break and reconnect and sometimes they just break and the growth here is learning when to let go when you need to.

***

A friend is someone who knows all about you, doesn't judge you and still loves you

TRUE FRIENDS ARE hard to come by; in a lifetime you may only find a few. A few is plenty: to find solid friends whom you can trust, tell them all about you and they don't judge at all or speak behind your back is truly special.

As I've got older, I can count my real friends on one hand;

I feel proud of this. I have some solid people who know all about me, who accept me as I am completely and stick by me no matter what. In life we meet people who we think are our friends: some we feel we should still be friends with, some are friends you have because you want to fit in, but half the time spent with these people you are not being true to yourself – we have all been here, I'm sure.

It takes strength to be true to yourself, to not go along with the crowd.

When I am around my close friends, I can be me. I don't need to hide my thoughts or opinions, we can disagree. I don't need to dress up all the time, wear make-up, pretend to know things I don't. I don't need to listen to people say bad things about others out of jealousy or spite.

From young we form friendships, discovering and learning. Friendship can be hard, at times we will hurt, feel let down, cast aside for a new model, friends you thought were friends won't care when it truly matters. Instead, we must nurture those friends with whom we will have numerous laughs and memories with. That friend you can pick up the phone to and know whatever it is, they have the time. Those friends who will be there unconditionally.

We all experience this, it's part of our growth. It's the lessons we take from this that heal us along the way and in the end, all that matters is that you are left with the friends who know the real you and care for you: you are left with the right ones.

Try not to judge or make assumptions when friends let you

down: they may simply not have the strength to be there for you in the way they once were. They may be carrying their own baggage which they are trying to heal themselves from and simply can't give anything back at this time. Or possibly the time you were meant to share is now over.

Those who are meant to stay, will.

***

When you judge others, you do not define them, you only define yourself. – **Wayne Dyer**

Lean into who you are, what you know and see what you see, fully!

***

As MANY TIMES as you can remember: come back to love, to you!

I have spent a lot of time constantly checking my phone for a sign that somebody cares. To know I'm in someone's thoughts. Feeding the self-doubt, the lack of confidence rising once more. In fact, I have spent so much time lost in thought about what other people think that I lost sight on many occasions of what I even wanted; again, lost in somebody else's ideal or dream. I also appreciate the older I get that we all have things going on, challenges, heartache and many people don't even wish to talk about their trauma. Somebody can be smiling each time you see them and then go home in a heap, burnt out, not able to send that message or check in on you. This doesn't mean they don't care. It's healthy to detach from this way of thinking and being, taking responsibility fully for you and how you feel is in my opinion a huge beneficial step to staying on the heart's path. You will come back over and over, and each time learn something new. Getting to know yourself a little more each time, finding the reconnection and even being happy in your own company.

Lunch for one!

As I sit here writing, I'm having lunch for one, finding peace aside the river. More often now the time I seek is alone; no external noise or distraction taking me away from myself, no company required. I never saw myself spending moments like this; pleasure found in enjoying my own presence. Life continues to show me that things do constantly change, even if we think they may not. It's funny really, as I've always clung on to an outcome, false security sought in the ideal of things being a certain way; now I find myself able to flow just like the river at times, no longer in need of conclusion. Asking myself, 'What does my heart need?'

Critical self-talk has been regular for me throughout life, especially when not completing what I'd set out to start or wading through what I planned to do quickly enough. Focused on the finish line I never appreciated the ride; I didn't want to! I wanted a busy mind so as not to think about everything else, all those fears sat just below the surface, I didn't want to give them space to take over; endless control seemed smart! However, by ignoring the anxieties, they were doing just that, taking over! By seeing them and exploring the challenging pathway, it's what led me to greater understanding. Now I can see just how much I gain as I wander. The voyage is not where I end up but, in the steps taken, in the love felt, in the truths listened to. So much insight sat within each experience yet so often missed in the longing. The ending is not too important, more so I see that adventures finish where needed and space becomes available for the next one to begin. We can't all follow the same route for it would get congested.

I've never been a 'stick to the track' kind of girl, even when seeming to need control of everything, I see that the outcome would never have panned out the way it may have set to look on paper and this all part of it. Just like the weather, we change, circumstance alters frequently and each day I'm more accepting of this natural unfolding. Exploring life in a more mindful fashion I find myself exploring the adventure, the new constant a path of discovery, not the need for control. Not only to the external things in front of my eyes either but also with what lies within myself. The more I notice; the more I uncover; the more I heal; and then the more I notice again. The loop continues and the emotions flow with it. Currently I sit within a sea of tears. It's mid-July – a new moon looming. I'm a Cancerian so it's no surprise the water flows freely. It's an ongoing process; a journey for sure but the acceptance creates freedom.

I often journal and often nothing feels finished but I now see that's ok. I released something I had to say, inspiration flowed for a while and then it stopped again. Just like my internal state of being, I glow for a moment like the sun and before I know it a heavy downpour again on its way. The rain falling, like the tears on my cheeks now dripping onto the page in front of me. Once more it settles for a while and then a thunderstorm takes hold; but this time, I stop, I watch and catch a moment of calm amidst this storm and it's here I find growth and meaning, I connect with my heart and get back on the path once more.

No matter how much we practise, life always

comes along. At times this can be turbulent but try not to judge it, if only for a second watch it. That's where the rainbow sits. The lesson and healing in the pause, the subtle crossover often missed.

Taking myself out for lunch today was quite a treat, it wasn't that I had no one to accompany me but more so that I didn't want any company and I loved being able to catch sight of those rainbows. I still enjoy time spent with others, but I no longer need company. Fewer diversions are present, less time spent watching Netflix, time once spent in endless interactions lost in something outside of myself now enjoyed in the simplicity of being by myself.

I noticed so much beside the river, I had time to be curious; even with the frustration of falling back into not achieving enough. But in waiting and watching I begin to see that so much is uncovered in just this. I've spent so much time looking for connection that I had lost the basic connection with myself.

So now when I don't know what to do or where to begin, I just let it all go, to let it all in. Each day, I'm simply doing the best I can; when I stop chasing, I now start receiving what's already here.

It is going to be all right you know; it may not feel like it, but it will. Things come along not only to illustrate where we've come from but to guide us to where we are going. Pay attention to where life leads you. Find meaning in each step. The rain can still be beautiful. We come through storms, often wiser than before. Learn from it all and when the sun comes again you can smile and see that you are here, you are strong, and you have already got through everything that's been thrown at you.

Here you come!

***

Keep facing the sun

To 'LOOK ON the brighter side of things' is something we have all likely been told before. Some days this can feel harder than others. We all have days feeling flat: the only thing you can do on these days is to be, nothing more. By allowing yourself to be, that's fine, that's still progress. It's important to not resist what you need – whatever that might be for you. Resisting can hold you back. Stopping keeps us connected to what we need. Pausing once more.

When things become difficult and you find it hard to pick yourself up, remember that taking rest is ok, you just do what you can; constantly achieving isn't the only way to move forward. Sometimes taking the pause propels you to where you need to be. Learn how to navigate your own compass.

Everything passes and if you take a break, you can still move forward. Permit yourself what you need in the moment you are in, don't give yourself a hard time.

There are meant to be struggles and obstacles in the way at times: moving through them when you are ready shows determination and the strength you have within. If you believe in yourself, you can make things happen when the time is right for you.

I often remind myself of what Roald Dahl said about keeping your face towards the sun, the way you are going is the next step forward. Yesterday has gone, it's ok to keep memories but don't hold yourself back there. Just like the shadows, let them fall behind you, becoming part of your being, your growth. Look forward to what's coming. Don't feel bad for feeling the sun on your face. Shadows can still be present but you don't have to live in them any more. The shadows are part of the growth; nothing sits in sunshine all day long.

Your future is out there waiting for you: don't resist it, just take each day at a time. There is no rush but keep believing and facing towards your dreams. Let the magic stir inside of you, let love show the way forward. Allowing everything to unfold in its own time, knowing the door is always open.

***

For the only way out is through!

We must move through difficulty in our own time, asking for help along the way if we need.

I have realised that since making these changes and approaching what I face in a mindful way, not feeling embarrassed to ask for a little help when required, I can now move through – baby steps, but I'm no longer glued to the start line! I get to notice my journey along the way rather than miss it. I reconnect to what matters and once more listen to my heart.

If you're struggling it can help to look from a place of non-attachment. To remove the personal and take an angle as though talking to a friend. By doing this we can tackle the issue itself instead of letting the emotion and pain cloud this opening, preventing access. Emotion will still rise naturally, but from a place of understanding rather than fear.

As your start to implement mindful awareness of how to analyse your behaviours and responses, you will gain confidence and in time begin to feel safe and secure. It's from this place you can navigate the best you can through the obstacles you might face. Difficult times come to teach us; lessons are always being learnt.

This path is yours to walk: keep grounded, stay open, stop and listen to what you have to say, listen to your heart, keep dreaming, take one step at a time – the guidance will come.

Mountain Calling

I see it in the distance, the mountain calling me,
A gentle wave within the breeze, guiding to be free.
I don't know how to get there, or what I'm supposed to do,
I trust in what I feel inside; my gut it feels it too.

Removing all attachment, nowhere for me to hide,
What does my life look like with nobody by my side?
Always seeking validation through other people's eyes.

Never showing all of me, a part held back, but why?
People-pleasing, fitting in, I continue, and I try.
A lack of worth and love for the person that is me,
Afraid to bear my heart and soul, shy away from humility.

Connecting deeper every day, uncertainty reduced,
I have all I need inside of me; much love and all my truths.

My breath it holds me once again, imposter at
the door,
I'm bare and fully open now for what I came
here for.

I no longer want to be second, a burden or a
chore,
I see it now: my beauty, my soul it calls for more.
For I can feed it what it needs, I have it all within,
Being true to who I am, no longer seen a sin.

***

Chapter 8

Mountain Calling

I DIDN'T REALLY understand this chapter myself when pulling the lessons together that I had learnt, all I knew was it had to be in here. These poems would just come to me, and this poem was part of my journey; I just hadn't worked it all out yet. Over the course of a few months, three events occurred that helped me understand why I felt so connected to the words that had flowed onto the page.

The first was when I was watching *Moana* for about the hundredth time with my youngest daughter – we all loved this film. She sat next to me and said, 'I want to be by the sea.' 'Me too,' I replied. We both smiled as little Moana gets caught in the wave and it styles her hair, pure joy as the wave places the flower in her hair. Then there's the scene where Moana is in the sea, singing 'I Am Moana (Song of the Ancestors)'.

It is inside me: all the answers I search for, that call from my soul, from my heart. It was never out there at all. Goosebumps, all over. I realised, just this, that's where it is:

the mountain calling, the song from inside my heart, my path, the lessons – it all swirled into one clear message, and I knew what it meant. I cried. I did know the way forward: come what may, I have the answers inside me and so do you.

The second moment of unveiling the connection to this poem was quite a few months later. I was at an aroma reiki session and at the end when I asked if anything had come up, the therapist explained what had come up for her: I was like a light surrounded by people and a choice of paths were laid before me – four in fact. She asked me which path I would like to choose. She didn't even need to say as I knew what was coming. Her words followed: 'You chose the mountain path.' We both knew it was calling me to it.

The third thing that happened in relation to understanding my draw to the mountain was meeting a lovely lady at a wellbeing sharing evening. I was drawn to her immediately and the following week we met up, where she brought me a shell with a hole in it and said I could wear it. She didn't know why she'd brought it, but she just did. I went to say about the Moana moment, and just before I opened my mouth, she said, 'I just feel a connection with Moana or something.' Once more I knew I had to trust myself with these callings.

I feel that the point of this short chapter is a reminder to us all that we have everything inside of us to move through all we face, coming back to who you are, reconnecting with you and showing yourself love and compassion, being open to the gifts and guidance a whole manner of people can provide you with. Discovering so much along the way and still going. I am so grateful for the twists and turns I have taken, or I wouldn't be here today. The mountain keeps calling, that peak within my heart and I keep following the call, day by day, step by step.

***

How do you know what your calling is?

REMEMBER THE POWER of the pause. And the power of saying no. Do you give yourself permission to stop? To be present, not overloaded with everything you feel you 'must' do?

You may feel guilty for stopping and taking a bit of time for you. The gentle pause of our breath is often missed but sitting in this space gives clarity.

There will always be things that need doing, but you have the power to stop and give yourself a break if you need. I used to resent others relaxing or taking time to stop and have a break, simply because I never allowed the same for myself. Reaching burnout meant I had to stop; there was no other choice. Sometimes we create distractions, keeping ourselves busy to avoid other things which we'd rather not face – for me, my anxiety. Looking back, the only person stopping me having time for me, being me, was me!

Create your path, fill some of your time with what you enjoy, your passions and don't feel guilty for it.

***

Options

In life we will all have an abundance of options available to us, in turn the choices we make lead us to where we are today.

Sometimes we may feel stuck, anxious, overwhelmed or lost, but there are always other options available, different choices. You may just need to slow down to see what your options are. Too often we miss opportunity; we miss what's already right here by always rushing.

By slowing down, the options available to you become clearer. When paying attention to what you are doing, being present, you can see things which were possibly lost amongst thoughts and emotions. We then start to see more of those *glimmers,* not just the *triggers*!

Allow yourself to see all the options within your reach, feel into who you are and what you want. Each day see if you can:

- Take some time.
- Notice what you're doing.
- Listen to how you feel.
- Take a few extra moments to wake up.
- Be aware of your body.
- Pay attention to the small things.
- Make no judgements of how it should be.
- Choose to not be concerned by what others think.
- Slow down.

The options we have and choices we make shape our experiences and lives to where we are today.

No matter what is happening around us, we always have a different option available if we don't like the way things are. The first step can just be changing the way you think – after all, 'thoughts become things'. We can choose how we react to any situation.

***

Dream ...

The person with big dreams is more powerful than one with all the facts. – **Albert Einstein**

NEVER GIVE UP on what you really want to do.

Do you remember your dreams? Do you live your dreams? Do you dare to dream?

We all have dreams, but don't always remember them. It is thought our most intense dreams happen during the REM (rapid eye movement) sleep cycle, which we experience several times each night. Our first dream usually happens after the first ninety minutes of sleep, but each night we have many.

What are our dreams trying to tell us? Are our dreams a guide, an insight?

Dreams are commonly considered as a window into the unconscious mind – creating a gateway between this and our conscious.

Always listen to your intuition, follow your heart; dreams can come true. Whatever your vision, make today part of that dream. Lean in.

Don't be pushed around by the fears in your mind. Be led by the dreams in your heart. **— Roy T. Bennett**

***

'The best dreams happen when you're awake' **— Cherie Gilderbloom**

We have so much in front of us, all around us. Can you make today, your reality, your life, part of your dream?

It's possible to live a life you once dreamt of.

Being awake, learning the true art of fully living is special. To live like this, is living the dream. Living in the present moment and not being caught up is magical: have you experienced this? Appreciating what's right here, now.

Dare to dream the impossible and live it. Feel it happening. Really see what others can't believe.

Your dreams can be felt in each day. Make your dreams your life.

See your dreams today: feel them, love them, live them.

***

Discover

WHO AM I beyond mum, partner, daughter, sister, friend, colleague?

Self-discovery unearths the bravery to start a hidden adventure that's been waiting for you all along, so start exploring right there. Small, subtle changes in every day.

Practising mindfulness and having this time during lockdown I discovered what I actually like doing, what I'm passionate about, how much I enjoy writing, meditating, dancing, seeing friends and family, baking and more.

If you give yourself a moment, some space, there is a whole world to discover. The adventure starts with you.

How does it make you feel when you discover something?

That excited feeling finding hidden treasures on the beach to fill your bucket. Discovering something new that you love that you never even thought you'd like. A great restaurant with good food.

Coming across a new song, a new fact, new ideas, a quirky little crystal shop!

One of the best for me is when you discover old things, bringing back precious memories – or better still discovering something new in something or someone that's been right there all along, you just hadn't seen it before.

How great it is when you discover a new book, you're completely sucked in, you are in that book – you can't put it down!

A beautiful new spot in nature you've never seen before. There is so much to discover – we just need to stop and look.

***

Last summer I did a mindful exercise. It was to take a mindful walk outside. No phones, no distractions, just myself. It was a boiling hot day, I was melting! I half didn't want to go as I was so hot. I stood in the paddling pool we had set up in the garden to cool down first, put my flip flops on and decided to walk round the block, the block I have walked a million times! Without my children, my dogs, my partner, my phone … it was such a peaceful feeling. I was aware of everything, including how little headspace I usually got. I noticed houses I hadn't seen before. I felt my feet on the ground, the heat, every bump, dip, the change in surface beneath my feet. I discovered a lot on that walk, things I had never seen. I also discovered I needed more time to be me, to discover who I am.

***

If on this adventure you feel resistance, or things feel a little tough during your own discovery, I wanted to share this with you to help ease that struggle, give it a try:

Hoʻoponopono

THE HAWAIIAN WORD Hoʻoponopono means to put things back into balance. 'Making the right righter'.

The translation comes from hoʻo ('to make') and pono ('right'). The repetition of the word pono means 'doubly right' or things being right with both self and others.

How to use Hoʻoponopono:

You acknowledge: 'I'm sorry'.
Ask for forgiveness and accept what is done: 'Please forgive me?'
Be grateful and move on: 'Thank you'.
Then share love: 'I love you'.

I'm sorry.
Please forgive me.
Thank you.
I love you.

If you really want to embody Hoʻoponopono the way I like to, full of emotion, here is my suggestion.

Take a moment, think of what you wish to heal, to let go of, to forgive and play this song: 'Carrie Grossman - Thank you.'

Close your eyes, enjoy!

Share 'Aloha' - Aloha has a deep meaning to the people of Hawaii, beyond its common use of 'hello' and 'goodbye'. Aloha also means kindness, affection and love. I know I want to bathe in Aloha!

This can be used for anything and everything and as many times as you like.

Give it a try.

Lean in

Lean into what you're feeling, there is no need to hide,
Heartbeat strong, connection felt, arms now open wide.
Things are really shifting, there's movement in my soul,
The energy, the power, it lies in letting go.

Freeing up my body, making space for what's to come,
The rhythm in my footsteps shine underneath the sun.
My vibe is rising higher now, seen underneath the moon,
I'm open and I'm ready, not a moment too soon.

Moving with the wind, my body like the trees,
Grounded and so stable, but room to still be free.
Out there in the quantum, already waiting there,
Rise to meet the frequency … it's mine if I dare.

***

Chapter 9

Lean in

I WANT TO begin with this quote.

Letting there be room for not knowing is the most important thing of all. **– Pema Chödrön**

It hasn't happened for a while but out of nowhere it hit me quite hard. Of all places – on a lovely break by the sea when I 'should' be relaxing. (Not a fan of the word should, more so trying to switch this to some recent advice, 'I could if I wanted to!') So, trying to relax and, out of nowhere, that same familiar feeling struck: unsettled and anxiety rising once more – just like that break with my girlfriends in Benidorm.

A series of small events had sent me into an unexpected anxious panic spiral.

The feeling of dread took over and the tears rushed down my face. The difference was, this time I didn't hide it, nor push it away. I was open and honest with how I felt and sat with it in a wide-open space, letting there be room for not knowing. By leaning in and being open with how I felt I was able to step out of the anxiety much quicker. No shame about it, just being with it.

By doing this, before too long I was able to detach from the panic I'd clung on to and could step back and see that I was feeling let down in a few areas in life. I had momentarily slipped into 'not feeling good enough', following a few things that had come up over the past weeks, and just like that anxiety rushed in.

That's the thing I now see a lot: we assume that when things are all wonderful that there is no room for error but it's often when we are sailing along without a care in the world that the capacity to access our feelings hits. One last small thing adding fuel to a fire that has been burning away, and the flames begin to roar.

I promise you, leaning in is the way out. Mindfulness, compassion, love and being with it; that's what brings changes, it brings healing. I'm braver now to sit with and be open with the problem, so moving through is easier. It's the whole reason I love sharing what I've discovered with others. Holding space to lean in. Having conversations and educating others around mental health as much as we can so we have the language to help and support each other.

During this unexpected period of heightened anxiety I was bowled over when my youngest daughter, eleven at the time, said this, 'Mum, what would you say? The fact you are aware of it means you aren't in it; you're observing it, so you're halfway out already!' WOW! Amidst the fear, the tears came, a mixture of pride, relief and release as the feelings of anxiety moved through.

If you don't hold space for what lies beneath it can get too heavy.

***

Meditation really has helped me become more myself, it has helped me find my way back to who I am! – **Anon**

FOR ME, THIS has been my experience, which is why I love this quote and wanted to share.

- Do you feel you are all of you?
- Who are you?
- Do you know you? What you really want and what things really matter to you?

Meditation helps us explore being with ourselves, creating self-awareness. It helps us observe our thoughts and not become them. Meditation lays the pathway back to us and creates the space to connect within. The more this is practised the more connected you become.

Living mindfully has taught me to be with whatever. Now I'm starting to trust whatever comes up.

Why do we second guess and question ourselves over and over? The answer for me is lack of confidence and trust in ourselves. No self-belief. For some reason putting everybody else's needs above our own seems 'the right thing to do'. Putting ourselves first, listening to what we need is often pushed aside as selfish.

When we start believing in ourselves, we won't ask as many of these questions. We will know that simply doing what we need to do for us, removing ourselves from situations that don't serve us well is ok and simply what we need to do. Looking after ourselves as we would others is a great principle to live by!

***

MEDITATION HELPS YOU lean into whatever is present.

I had tried to meditate quite a few times over the years but always got frustrated that I wasn't able to do it 'correctly' or hadn't reached a completely clear and still mind. Or wasn't always seeing beautiful colours or having strong visions. As a result I would not continue with it, out of judgement of doing it wrong (the thing that holds us back from many things!). Some time would pass and I'd be drawn back to it again for the same thing to happen. It wasn't until I tried it again after my final burn out that I really got it and have been meditating mostly every day ever since.

Notice what you notice …

I heard this during a guided meditation and it really struck a chord within me, and I thought, *I can do this*. So, I started off with just a few minutes of noticing and bringing my awareness back to my breathing. Then my mind would wander off again and I would be aware of spotting my mind wandering and bring it back all over again. In time, I extended a couple of minutes to five, then ten, fifteen, twenty, sometimes longer if I felt like it or had the time. It became easier and easier, my mind clearer. For me this was one of the biggest eye-openers and changed my whole relationship with meditating, so if you're new to meditating, I hope this helps you too.

I still attend group meditations now and others reflect saying they reached stillness or had an array of colours but I now see that everyone's experience is different and each meditation for me is different. I don't do the same amount each day and I don't have the same experience each time but that is all part of it.

What I do know is that I now don't like going without it and whatever experience I have will benefit me. When I don't take time to listen, to lean in, I notice the adverse effects of not paying attention.

If you haven't tried meditation but want to, or have had a similar experience to me, remember: just notice what you notice.

***

MUSIC SOFTENS THE pain, it can help you move through it, feel the emotion. It also increases the joy and opens the heart. Mindfulness of music itself is magic, you can be so present with a song. You can meditate with the music itself, aware of the different sounds, the vibrations, the frequency.

You can observe the feelings felt and where you feel them in the body. Notice and lean into whatever emotions are present through this experience too.

Music is so powerful, music itself has healing powers. Have you ever had a bad day and then you put the radio on and a song that you love starts playing? How good is that feeling! All the joy flowing around your body at the sound of it – your energy changing. The huge influence music has on us all in different ways is amazing. It enables expression and helps communication through the music itself.

Music brings me so much: memories, freedom, healing, relaxation, motivation, better sleep. It gives me a reality check, it's relatable. It softens the pain and increases the joy. It can boost my whole day; it can cradle my heart if it's hurting. Being able to dance to different styles of music releases stress and enables expression through movement. Worldwide we all enjoy this pleasure. Music can transport you to memories and bring them to life. Music brings people together.

It has been found that music stimulates the brain more than any other human function. It's not surprising how many positive effects it has. Helping study, sleep, relaxation, fitness, memory, positivity, happiness and so much more. It can even ease pain and manage stress!

The power of music can open your heart as you hear, relate and feel open. Such a beautiful, powerful thing.

Put your favourite song on today – soften your pain, increase your joy and open your heart.

***

SYNCHRONICITY STRUCK AS this quote by Pema Chödrön popped up:

Things falling apart is a kind of testing and a kind of healing. We think the point is to pass the test or to overcome the problem, but the truth is that things don't really get solved. They come together and they fall apart. Then they come together again and fall apart again. It's just like that. The healing comes from letting there be room for all of this to happen: room for grief, for relief, for misery, for joy.

The more honest and open you are, the less fear you will have.

***

CONNECTING WITH BEING honest can be hard, being open can be difficult, but leaning into whatever comes up will help you break through rather than break down. These things are often only a challenge to us because we put pressures and judgements on ourselves, which causes fears and anxiety.

Once we see who we are, when we are completely comfortable in our own skin and we are honest with ourselves, it's easier to be honest with others. Opening up and leaning in is brave: being completely true to yourself, accepting your fears, your flaws with as much acceptance as your wonders. Once accepted, you see that every part of your being is as important as the next and you start to understand that everything you have been through has brought you to this place and was required for you to fully flourish into who you are today.

When you are authentic with yourself you are no longer anxious about the mask slipping, revealing the real you: living authentically means you have revealed yourself already.

Be strong, love who you are – all of you, every part, each scar, misfortune, each achievement as part of what makes you, you!

***

MINDFULNESS AND MEDITATION have really helped me find the place inside myself where I now think nothing is impossible. You must find that place inside yourself too. I may have hurdles ahead and at times I only manage to take small steps but I'm trusting myself and moving forward.

We all have this place inside of us, we just can't find it at times. Much of the time it's most likely hidden beneath the layers of fear and self-doubt we've built up around ourselves.

Having confidence and trust in yourself is so important; something I have lacked for a long time. I love giving advice and encouraging others to have no fears and do their best but when it comes to myself, I often have doubt. Why do we do this? But when we begin to peel back the layers, the confidence grows.

We can all dream. If we believe in it and take that chance, it can become reality. Lean into what you're feeling and take the first step.

***

You are beautiful just the way you are!

I AM INCREDIBLY lucky to have two beautiful, strong, independent daughters. I often question if I have done enough, been enough, shown up enough and all the other questions we have when being a parent, but as time goes on, I see that many of the worries I had over the years weren't important at all. Being a few minutes late, missing the alarm, forgetting a World Book Day, not packing a water bottle, a sunhat … this list could go on for a very long time, but the thing is, none of these things matter. Love, that's what matters. Time, listening, love! That's when happiness is felt.

One evening, my daughter said to me before bedtime, 'Mum, you are so beautiful.'

Feeling not the most attractive, no make-up worn at all (this had become my default), living in the most casual, comfy clothes whilst carrying a little extra weight I suddenly felt great, despite not such a glamorous look. This comment making me feel so happy, I was made up. Not in make-up; in happiness. I think it was Drew Barrymore who said the best form of make-up is happiness. It is! It lifts your mood and you shine from inside – all your natural beauty glowing. Once more connected to you, your heart; to love.

Not worrying about what you look like, or feeling you need validation from what size clothes you wear, what shape you are etc. We often veer off the path trying to fit in. Some will judge a person's beauty, their own beauty or image, what's on the outside, but it's only the surface. When you really see somebody, their heart, their soul, nothing can match that. That lights up a room like fireworks in the sky.

Everyone has a different perception of beauty and will see beauty in different ways, in different things. This doesn't make anyone any less beautiful than the next person. We find happiness in our own way and to me both happiness and beauty come back to love.

Look at yourself today: see how beautiful you are. Show yourself some love.

Sharing happiness, spreading happiness: this is what makes the world beautiful, makes us beautiful.

Put your make-up on in the form of a smile. Everyone around you won't just see your beauty, they'll feel it!

The most uplifting thing I've discovered is to give myself a chance and appreciate me – all of me, just as I am. To see all the beauty inside and out, the scars, stretch marks, the tears, the bad days – they are all part of my story too.

When you lean right in and become comfortable with who you are, confident in your own skin, others feel that radiate; it's beautiful. Having appreciation of your own beauty, including the imperfections, enables everything you look at to become enhanced in this beautiful light too.

Self-criticism is something we all do: we judge the way we

look, what we should wear, how we behave, what we should and shouldn't do. It's draining! It's also unhealthy to do so. Why do we criticise ourselves so much?

Don't try and change who you are, try and *find* who you are instead. Be curious, ask yourself questions. Look how far you've come, see how strong you are.

What is important to you?

You may lack confidence, have self-doubt, but you don't need to: you are beautiful just the way you are. Start noticing this; start noticing you. To appreciate everything you see you must love and accept everything within.

Being you – that is beautiful!

***

Shine like the beams from the sun, be authentically you

Good thoughts produce good feelings, in turn you feel better and attract what will serve you to remain authentic. Do you notice this uplifting change when having good thoughts? Your smile and cheerful outlook become infectious, your presence shining. When you are happy and thinking positively you can feel it.

Our mindset is an incredible resource: when thinking positively your overall wellbeing is enhanced. Positive thinking reduces stress and depression, having these good thoughts more regularly promotes healing.

A great way to practise positive thinking is through affirmations.

Try these affirmations, repeating each one three times to yourself:

- I am a positive person.
- I love my body.
- I am confident.
- I have so much love and support.
- I am enough just as I am.

Appreciating the good things around you, no matter how small they are, promotes good thoughts. Positivity is contagious: shine and watch others shine with you. With a smile on your face, you feel lifted immediately.

***

Free your mind

OUR MINDS ARE filled daily with thoughts, fears, must-dos and should-haves.

The importance of freeing your mind. Something so simple but we often don't allow the space for it; why not?

Being consumed to excess is unhealthy and it's important

we give ourselves space to free our minds from overload in our ever-busying world. We make time for so much but too often neglect ourselves.

Allow your mind to wander: simply take a purposeful pause, don't resist anything, just let it all be. Breathe, and remember, freeing your mind doesn't mean no thoughts!

***

Do you know how to listen to your intuition? Do you trust your intuition? Your gut feeling, your intuition is usually right. Sadly, we don't trust it some or much of the time – usually due to unhelpful patterns we've learnt over time. Opening up to our intuition, listening to ourselves often holds the answers we search everywhere for, we just need to listen. The more we do, the louder the voice.

Our intuition is situated in our sixth chakra, our third eye. (See the Mindful Moments section at the back of the book for brief guidance on each chakra.) Being intuitive means having a knowing about something, but we don't always trust our intuition; why is this? Should we? This is something I am extremely interested in and am trying to learn more about.

To tune into your intuition you must be fully present; once in tune it can be so powerful.

Meditation enables you to strengthen your intuition. Through meditating, I have discovered how it opens you up further to connect with your intuition and have trust in this.

If you take some time in silence and enable peace for your mind, your intuitive voice will indeed become louder. You will then receive guidance to be able to be truer to yourself and listen.

Have you ever had a gut feeling, a strong pull to something or a voice telling you something? This is your intuition: it guides you to your higher self. Through this you can communicate between your body and soul, enabling you to find your life purpose and connect with your dreams.

It is wonderful and there is so much to explore. I'm excited to be on this journey and I want you to be excited too.

Trust your intuition: it's the ultimate act of trusting yourself.

Trust your gut – follow whatever it is today that feels right, don't push it away.

***

QUITE OFTEN INTROVERTED people are seen as those who don't want to be around people. They are also much quieter, preferring to be more reserved much of the time. Introverted behaviour often means the capacity to listen is high, versus the amount wished to be spoken. Interestingly, it is thought that a higher percentage of people are the opposite: they are extroverted, happy to speak up and be in social situations.

I have read about the different types of people in this regard and thought about most people I know when looking into this. Some people I can't define one way or the other, including myself. I believe my family and friends would say I am an extrovert (being quite chatty, appearing confident and willing to help, to go first). Yet, for me, looking inward was the beginning of finding myself. And the more I read about introverts, the more I see how I have become comfortable being this way too.

Do you have to be one way or another? Or can you be both?

What would you say you are? Are you an ambivert? I also wonder, do you change or adapt over time?

Whilst making the connections from what I have studied so far about these behaviours, and understanding fully the different personalities, I've concluded that there are many different possibilities within whatever type or personality you may be, and it's hard to sometimes define exactly what this is.

To look inward is the beginning of finding yourself.

By being quiet you hear more, so at points we all need to be introverted to connect within and be in silence. In silence we can listen deeply and tune into ourselves and others, which I feel I am able to do, but am I fully listening?

I am now completely comfortable with focusing on my inner thoughts, spending time by myself and being with just a few close people. I like being free of interruption, being able to feel and sense what I need. I also like to listen to, think and hear about what others have to say.

But I still love being around lots of people. I like discussing how I feel and enjoy meeting new people. I am confident in a social setting and love going out. I've read much on introverted behaviour and now assume – rightly or wrongly – that we are all this way on some level, and we may just hide from this particular label, as it appears to have (unnecessary) negative connotations at times.

***

In the process of letting go, you lose things, but you will find yourself – **Deepak Chopra**

Do YOU WANT to feel and experience all the wonderful things that are meant for you in this life? See and be all the things that are meant to be?

I know I do. I want to make space for it all and release what I no longer need. Sometimes this may be hard to do but to fully find yourself, letting go is part of the process. Even if it's something simple like feeling the need to put the washing on as soon as I get up or sorting out my cup immediately after a cup of tea. Or a harder challenge: letting go of guilt for not spending time with people I feel I should, but who don't make me feel good about myself at all. Now I see it is ok to let go of this obligation, for the good of myself.

Letting go of these old patterns, habits and even people from the past really is creating space for me, even making the time to write this, which I love. I would have not allowed myself the time previously due to filling up my day with all the things I thought I 'should' be doing. Well, today I choose to overlook the mountains of jobs in front of me and spent a moment writing this!

Let go, lean in, find you.

The more I let go, the better I feel ...

Does fear hold you back every single time?

Why didn't you make that call?

Go for that job?

Start a new hobby?

Not say how you really felt?

Had belief you could do it?

Stand up for yourself?

Speak your view?

Take the next step?

Walk away?

Fear prevents us from doing so much. Of course, at times it prevents us from real danger. But increasingly, much of the time this fear is just misinformation or thoughts we tell ourselves that aren't helpful at all. Much of the time these things aren't even happening. Fixating on the what ifs and maybes just prevents us from living.

***

You MAY HAVE read it before:

False
Evidence
Appearing
Real

This is what happens: our minds are so powerful we convince ourselves that these threats are things, that we shouldn't do them, the thoughts take over. By paying attention we allow this to happen, blowing everything out of control, making the fear bigger.

Sometimes genuine fear will be present, but if we always run away from fear or try and take control of it, we will never be at ease with it.

Don't let fear stand in your way. You are just as capable as the next person – you've just got to believe it can happen, and it will.

Don't let fear hold you back this time!

***

Wherever you are right now, that's where you're supposed to be!

Do YOU FEEL you need to rush forward?
That you should be doing more?
Do you wish you were somewhere else?

If something bad or unwanted arises do you try and push these thoughts or the situation away?
Do you fully engage in all the wonder and joy you experience?

Pressuring ourselves all the time, trying to keep up, or wanting to do things we've done in a different way just takes enjoyment away from our journey and it makes it harder to process what comes up for us as we have too many factors in the way.

This road we are on won't be the same as the next person's and it won't ever be plain sailing – as well as joy, laughter and excitement, there will be sadness, pain and loss. We can't grow without accepting it all; sometimes we must allow ourselves to just be with what is without pushing it away, and this hurts.

Sometimes the right decisions hurt people, but a time comes when you know what's right and you trust yourself. We are all exactly where we are meant to be in this moment; we mustn't pressure ourselves to be somewhere else or try and be someone else.

The happy moments become more visible when we are truly present. Removing all expectations of 'our idea' of what should be or how we should react creates freedom.

If you need to laugh, that's ok.
If you need to cry, that's ok.
If you need to grieve, allow it.
If you need to do nothing, this is ok too.

Keep asking yourself questions!

There is no rule book on life. One life won't fit all but walking your own path in your own time doesn't make this wrong. It makes it your journey and that's where you are meant to be right now.

The hard times teach us, they enable growth. The good times bloom from this. Being present with each emotion fully allows more freedom in the mind, more freedom in your life.

Some things are simply out of our control: let these things go, don't let them take away from what is here for you today. It doesn't mean don't feel it, just simply let go of trying to control it. Remember, the power is in the response. That's the only thing you can control; let the rest be as it is.

Don't put added pressure on yourself on top of the things you already have to deal with by trying to be someone you're not.

You're enough as you are, enjoy what is yours. Be true to you – in this moment and the next.

Encourage

ENCOURAGE OTHERS ALWAYS, share positivity and hope they can believe in themselves too.

- Never forget to encourage yourself too; you can do all you are meant to achieve.
- Completely have faith in your abilities.
- Continually show your encouragement and support.
- Underestimate nothing at all: you are capable!

- Radiate your energy to everyone around you.
- Adapt if you need to, you will reach your goals.
- Go after what you want, you'll be the only thing holding you back.

We all see things differently

WE ALL LOOK at things differently and perceive them in our own way. We may even look at the same object on a different day and see it as something else. It's ok to have your own path, we don't all walk the same way. We all must face change every day, change is constant and sometimes hard to face.

Sometimes change may bring sadness but with change there may be new opportunity. Accepting change and having a mindful attitude to change allows you to free yourself from aspects of it. You don't have to like the change; just notice how you feel about it.

Observe your thoughts (remembering we are not our thoughts, we feel them). By taking a moment to be the observer it will help you work out a healthier way to move forwards.

***

Some people feel the rain, others just get wet – **Bob Marley**

I LOVE THIS quote. Not only is his music amazing but I find so much truth and meaning in his words. They make me look deeper within.

Do you feel the rain? Really feel it? Or do you just get wet? I certainly used to just get wet – and moan about it too! Now I feel it, and what a difference it makes.

This applies to anything. We so often rush through life, not feeling much of what we could, experiences passing us by, people growing older around us. Not grabbing hold of that chance when it presents itself.

Take a moment today to feel the rain, really lean in and notice what you're feeling. The comfort you may get from something as simple as your evening meal. How good does it feel when you come in from a long walk in the cold, you're so hungry, that warm meal you're about to eat in front of you. Do you just eat it so fast it's gone, or do you taste it, slow down, tune into how that meal makes you feel?

Music, a song you love. The sound of a good tune, the feel-good vibes, your body alive with the rhythm and the words you can hear; you can feel! Time spent with someone close to you. A FaceTime or phone call with someone you enjoy conversation with. How does that make you feel? We can make the calls, put the music on and cook the food but do we truly feel and enjoy these things as we could?

There is so much to feel, but if you don't take some time to enjoy these things you will just remain wet, never drying off, and all the while moments you want to feel will pass you by.

I hope you feel some rain today.

***

Stay Open

A voice it sits inside me, wanting to speak up,
Yet I don't feel safe to, the audience is tough.
Trauma present for me, not even understood,
Can't find the words to ask for help, yet I wish
I could.

Instead escape feels easier, late nights, distraction
too,
Blocking it out is easier than trying to work it
through.
Embarrassment and shame around what's felt
inside,
If I raise my voice, and open up, then nowhere
left to hide.

Eventually I notice that freedom lies in love,
To listen with compassion, no longer try and
judge.
Allow it all to be there, acceptance is the key,
Take your time and feel it, for then you can be
free.

**

Chapter 10

Stay Open

BEING BRAVE ENOUGH to open up is tough. Staying open is challenging too, to keep sharing how you truly feel – despite the resistance that rises – yet it's essential to the freedom we seek. When dealing with mental health challenges – whether your own or those around you – it's not easy. I even recently spoke to somebody who said to me that until six years ago, he didn't even believe in mental health. I was so taken aback by this comment. For a very long time, I've had an increasing awareness around it, much of this due to circumstance I know, but for people in their forties to only be recognising mental health now left me a bit stumped. On the other hand, it helps me understand why historically it was so difficult to discuss and why, even just a few years ago, there wasn't healthy conversation or support. It wasn't really talked about and so that cycle continued. There is so much to learn about the varying types of mental health and struggles that each person individually goes through, but the more we stay open and talk about what's present, the more accepting we all become and in turn more support becomes available.

When my mum became unwell, it was unknown territory. Mental health and bipolar unfamiliar and not a talked about subject. In turn it wasn't really discussed by any of the family at all. My mum herself embarrassed by this and even now as I write I have those thoughts in the back of my mind. Will Mum and Dad be angry for me sharing my story, for writing how I feel? Well maybe they will at first and maybe they won't. All I know is, I see how important it is to talk about how we feel, to process our feelings and gain freedom from this. I constantly wonder why as a population we are so bogged down by the worry of what others think, how we will be perceived. What about how we see ourselves?

I've explored self-compassion vs shame several times now. Growing up there was a lot of shame around mental health. Very much stiff upper lip and get on with it, pull through and that's that. Expressing all the emotion and pain simply not welcome. When the difficulties had softened it was no longer spoken about. Once more 'just get on with it'.

I have shut down so many times, anxiety usually getting the better of me but the background niggle to release and open was always present. The thing was, for a long time my voice fell on unwelcome ears. My emotion too much, tedious, draining. Response always, 'Don't worry ... Don't cry.' So again, I would shut down. It wasn't until I started to explore more that I realised feeling was ok, it wasn't too much and actually quite healthy. We feel it anyway so making a little space to express it and release it made complete sense.

Difficult days followed, as I expressed a little bit, no longer pretending, just feeling what was present. *When is it ever going to end?* Relentless voices and questions in my head, but I went with it. I released, I wrote it out, meditated, shared how I felt where I felt safe and accepted, and gradually, I felt the change. I do feel the change. For some, I'm still just 'banging on', but it's ok, I now spend more time in spaces where I can safely release emotion, these important moments to express, something which is essential for us all. If you don't have the environment at hand to do this, you can cultivate one.

Sometimes life beats you down, but if we don't get back up, we can't grow. Not everyone will see you the way you want to be seen. Stood right in front of somebody's eyes, desperate to be loved, yet they see straight through you.

***

Today the sun was shining, it was a glorious day, yet I felt on edge when I woke up but couldn't put my finger on it. My old patterns were creeping in, and I could feel every sensation in my body. I didn't know why; life felt perfect right now. This is what happened sometimes, and it just caught up with me today it would seem. I had first started to suffer with anxiety soon after I had my first daughter. Until this point, despite the ups and downs I'd had growing up, I'd really kept a lid on things and was as carefree as they come … or so I thought. Back then my addiction not anxiety but other distractions. But now the responsibility of becoming a parent myself had instilled a slight sense of fear; protection almost.

Meditation seemed hard at first: always obsessing … I can't do this … I'm not doing it right! But then I noticed that (like with everything I tried, not just the meditation) I put so much judgement on my own life and the way things are done. If things were just accepted without judgement yet within reason things do flow far easier! The moment I realised there was no right way, things finally began to fall into place. We each have our own flow and that's ok. Far too much pressure in the world, on children, on families, on working, on how things should be. My take on the pandemic (when the world literally stopped as we knew it) changed what I thought things should look like and released pressure in many ways.

23 March 2020: The day the UK was put into lockdown, following suit of many other countries around the world. The lockdowns began in China, dripping through to other countries which at first seemed like distant news. When it reached Italy, things appearing bad I knew we were going to be hit hard. I'd always thought on the cautious side especially as I had suffered with anxiety. But despite all the energy I was throwing at remaining positive, deep

down I knew my wedding was never going to happen at the end of the month.

The news came on, Boris made his announcement and just like that, 23 March 2020, the UK lockdown began.

It was a strange day as so many had already prepared for it ahead of the announcement, the whole country seemed a mix of confused and fearful, knowing what was coming following the news Covid-19 had hit Europe. Weeks ahead of this day people everywhere were panic buying. You couldn't buy toilet roll for love nor money, hand soap and sanitiser too. Soon after this other items like pasta, tinned tomatoes, paracetamol, they were all running out in stores everywhere, online. It was crazy but you couldn't help but get sucked into the panic of it all. We closed our office Friday 20 March. I worked in a local estate agent, had for the past 12 years, we had many people in and out of the office and a week earlier had kept the doors locked to the public following advice. Some saying it's just like the flu, others panicking, each taking it for what it was. Everyone had to deal with this in their own way, no right way or wrong but we all had to pull through and try and rationalise the fear. The news was filled with coronavirus stories, largely negative and fear was being installed in everyone.

Schools had closed across England on Friday 20 March and when this was announced we all assumed it was serious. In my history, my parents' history, this had never happened. We chose to close the office the same day, having two children myself aged 7 & 13 at the time. I wanted to be with them. My partner and I worked together and knew we had the facility to set up from home, so that's what we did. Home schooling and working began and we set in to our new normal for the weeks ahead. Three weeks became six and fortunately the weather was warm.

I was quite fortunate: my family had their health and during this we remained well, aside usual colds and illness. My children were amazing. They managed lockdown with positivity, love and kindness. I couldn't be prouder. Their bond really strengthened, they played together, read together! They read so many books. My elder daughter couldn't put books down; she'd always loved reading but now her head was in books all the time. A mini-Matilda! She was so positive too, no anxiety or fear in the lockdown at all, she really took each day for what it was and enjoyed it.

She was my pillar of strength. My younger daughter followed her big sister with lots of reading, playing and coming into her own. She too my little inspiration. Having this time to watch my family grow and bond was changing me; everything changed.

My younger daughter, like me, had anxiety. Hers started at the young age of 6 when she had a nasty fall in year 2 and it wasn't dealt with very well. She had worried on and off, all the time getting worse as she moved up to her new school in year 3. Together we had read self-help books, workbooks and many things to try and tackle her anxiety (and mine at the same time, if I'm honest). Nothing helped like having the time to literally stop and breathe. It might sound silly, but I never had the time or at least didn't think I had the time before to do this. Now the world had literally stopped in its tracks and I could look at my family and see who they really were, appreciate everything about them.

We played so many games, card games really. Went on many bike rides, we had so much fun. I just loved them and who they were. They had always been there, all these wonderful things, but life moved too fast sometimes for me to be able to really take it in. I was so in awe of everything

I had and realised everything I needed was in front of me this whole time. The world had stopped, pollution reduced, waters clear, wildlife restoring, people pulling together. Each Thursday evening, we clapped the NHS. There was a real sense of togetherness and each Thursday that passed a real milestone: a week further ahead to the end of the lockdown. The first week, the evenings were still dark and just myself, my daughter and the lady across the street clapped together. The emotion was high, and I'll never forget that moment. The weeks went on and more and more neighbours came out, the evenings now lighter and families out together clapping, cow bells ringing, horns blowing. It was a real community feel. Although the news was filled with fear and negativity, the community was filled with love and spirit, and I was proud for my daughters to see this.

The whole world stopping was really something, flights grounded, people not able to see their friends or families in person. Zoom calls and classes taking over the world by storm! The wonder of the internet and technology.

Having this time to stop healed parts of me as well as the wildlife. All the while coming back to love and connection, new connections made.

Being open with my daughters about my anxiety really highlighted the importance of staying open, that it wasn't healthy to keep closing the doors (as I had previously). Their understanding and tremendous support has been so healing and freeing for us all. No need to constantly wonder, instead feel safe to just ask the question, say what's on your mind and discover the new doors in turn. If I hadn't had these forced pauses, firstly after my break in Spain and then again during lockdown I may not have kept the doors open and what a shame that would have been. The openness has led me to the most amazing places and in these spaces I have found the most amazing people waiting, with open hearts.

***

You are only limited by your ability to stay open –
Michael A. Singer

When I heard this, I gave it much thought. I had to think it over to get the full grasp of what I was learning (am still learning). How do we stay open? Are we not already open?

This revelation has been a transformation. It is so important to stay open, if we remain closed, we don't help anything at all, we just prevent the healing. We don't see or experience our whole self. It is natural that we want to protect ourselves from pain. When we have suffered hurt and hard times or betrayal it has often become a learnt behaviour to close off and put our walls up. The problem with doing this is we simply can't grow.

By being open it allows healing and spiritual growth. You can see your whole self; you see yourself with the eyes that see what you see. You hear what you know is right. If you want to be free you must be open. The need to remain open frees us.

Don't close your heart, allow yourself to be all of you, to be free, to grow, stay open.

Despite the setbacks, being knocked back or put down, trying again takes courage. Is there something you've always really wanted to do? Thought of doing but haven't had the courage? Had self-doubt? Thought you weren't good enough? Thought now is not the right time? All the above?

You are all that you believe, you can make the impossible, possible.

***

As I CONTINUE to take pause and reflect, I really notice my journey. Parts of life pass us by unnoticed and later can resurface without warning. I thought for a brief moment that I had it all together, life sorted, free from past cycles, free from those patterns I trapped myself in for a while. Then I find them arising again. Briefly losing grip on reality – detached from this moment. The good thing with mindfulness being a huge part of my life, my awareness kicked in and I could see and feel the signs once more. I also accepted that at times I experience feelings of anxiety, but I am not it. And day by day I learn to manage and it's ok, but each time I'm now so grateful that I can catch myself a little earlier and in turn come back to the present once more to where I am now.

Many wonderful things have happened for me this year, and some not so great. I am lucky to feel a lot of love and have some incredibly beautiful people in my life whom I couldn't be without, especially when things are not always plain sailing. I have drawn in some unexplainable pleasure and joy through being open and with it felt pain and sadness too but if I had to live my life over, I wouldn't change it. When we're brave enough to stay open our hearts find connection to what matters, to love. Feeling happiness wholeheartedly is wonderful. I also see that we make choices which may not be perfect but they're ours.

***

I AM FOREVER learning from others and find so much meaning in quotes: that one line sparks something inside and I open, I see a new insight.

I've always loved this quote but hearing it again recently, it rings true again.

In the beginner's mind your possibilities are endless, but with the expert's mind there are few. – **Shunryu Suzuki**

Every action, each decision, each choice has a message if we slow down and hear it – see it and feel it.

Change is scary, life is hard but if we never make time to

listen to ourselves, we lose a part of that and as we embrace the changes around us, it doesn't mean we have to change who we are; maybe we just slowly become a little more comfortable being who we already are.

***

Every single person on the planet has a story

RECENTLY WHEN ON holiday in Wales, sat alone on the beach looking out to the sea, a man with a frisbee caught my eye again. I'd seen him the day before and was intrigued by his commitment to this practice he repeated time and time again.

On this day, he continued to throw his frisbee into the wind, high up in the air, catching it every time. It was truly fascinating to watch. I got caught up watching him for some time and only when I heard the noise of my family coming to join me did I take my eyes off him.

'What are you doing, Mum?'

'I'm fascinated by the man with the frisbee. I'm trying to work out the reasoning behind his movement with his other arm,' I replied. The movement between each throw was the same each time, almost like one-sided tai chi. My family all proceeded with their own version and assumptions and judgements of this movement, with crazy far-fetched stories (some unkind) and then I declared, 'I'm going to ask him.' Each of them telling me not to and he could be a crazy man etc. Anyway, off I went across the beach, some distance away. I was just so intrigued. I approached him, introduced myself and said, 'I hope you don't mind, but I wonder, what it is you are doing with your left arm?' I'd taken note of him being right-handed and throwing the frisbee with this hand.

He informed me that if he didn't do left-hand movements he would be like a long-armed ape, as all the movement with throwing the frisbee was with his right arm, so he did this sequence in between to balance it out. It seemed to make a lot of sense and just goes to show not to judge the man as 'crazy'. I asked him what had brought him here …

To my amazement he started off with saying this, 'I'm just here, I come here each and every day and just be with my frisbee.' He shared some further insights on his life: he had five daughters (one adopted) and moved to Wales in 1974, living in caravans for twenty-five years. He commented on the extreme heat down there (it was a particularly hot August) and how he would just come and sit in the sea. Then he welcomed me to stand beside him. He said it's important to get the right wind and how he is always aware of the wind, its direction and speed, and that he'd like to give advice to wind surfers but he wouldn't. He said this with a toothless smile and drew my attention to his missing front teeth. He made me smile as he told me his front teeth weren't missing due to being knocked out by a frisbee, just down to old age. I told him I couldn't imagine a man with these skills would knock out his front teeth with a frisbee, and we smiled. He continued to throw the frisbee. I asked him what he does if dogs come along, seeing as they like to catch frisbees. 'I just time it right,' he replied. 'I'm always aware of what's happening in this moment.'

He said many other things, including the importance of having a 135 frisbee (a frisbee weighing 135 grams) and frowned upon the shops selling 175s. Not to use a frisbee with a hole in, only the solid kind. There is a small beach on Aberporth exceedingly difficult to catch the right wind. He had a bag with the tree of life on the front, with frisbees inside – old broken frisbees he used as ashtrays or ornaments.

I stood beside him for what felt like not long at all and before I knew it half an hour had passed, and I just watched the frisbee fly up and every time it came back. He was so present with this, right in this moment his meditation the frisbee itself. He was exactly where he was and he was ok with this, all his teeth missing but he was so happy … and with this in mind I want to share with you a meditation I wrote following my meeting of him … I hope this helps you open up to a little of the magic inside you. (If you prefer to listen to meditations, I have provided an audio recording for this; you'll find the link below.)

Frisbee meditation

So, CLOSE YOUR eyes now (if that feels comfortable) and really settle into your seat, noticing where you are now. Just breathing naturally and being present the best you can.

Be open to explore what arises for you today with fresh eyes and if possible, 'Letting there be room for not knowing, which is sometimes the most important thing of all.' And accepting that we won't always know the answers, but it's from this place we grow.

Breathing in – notice your body.

Breathing out – notice your thoughts. Not attaching to them, just simply being with what arises. Being here now.

Really connecting with your breathing now, taking that a little deeper if it feels comfortable and noticing any feelings or sensations in the body.

Bringing your awareness down to your feet now, notice how they feel, the soles of your feet, your toes ... wiggling them a little you sense your feet within the sand ... you're stood on the beach ... it's stretched out ahead of you ... and just beyond this the edge of the sea is in the distance.

You slowly begin walking towards the sea. With every step you feel the sand underneath your feet, between your toes; the soft white sand like a cushion underneath each step. You can hear the sea, the waves softly splashing as they draw in and that distant sound as they retreat. You hear birds above you and the wind blowing, a nice warm breeze.

You walk a little closer towards the shoreline and as you walk ahead you notice a frisbee on the ground. What colour is your frisbee? You smile as you reach down and pick it up. Notice how it feels as you grip its edges in your fingers. Now you walk a little closer towards the sea. You feel the wind once more and throw the frisbee up into the wind. Watch it leave your hand and come back down again, then as you catch it.

Again, just where you are, hold the frisbee in your hand and with the next throw think of what you want to let go of, what you may wish to release – again no right or wrong answer, just see what comes up. When the frisbee comes back, notice what's come with it. What you catch on its return, is it something new or something you tried to let go of?

Just be mindful of what comes up for you: release and bring a kind awareness to what returns to you. No judgement either way, just simply noticing what comes up for you currently.

Stand here a while longer and in your own time be with this practice a few moments more. Again, just noticing what is present for you.

When the time feels right, allow the frisbee to settle in your hand and when it feels comfortable just place it back on the sand beside you, hearing the sounds around you.

Slowly bring your attention back to your next breath, aware of where you feel this in your body and once more just be with where you are now and what has come up for you.

As you connect with your own breathing knowing: **There is nothing more than this moment.**

Just remembering: *Letting there be room for not knowing is sometimes the most important thing of all.* – Pema Chödrön

Take a moment to be here now.

And as we come to the end of this meditation now, bring your awareness to the sounds in the room around you, the temperature in the room. Bring some soft movement back to your body if that feels comfortable and when you're ready gently open your eyes.

How do you feel now?

Take a moment and spend a few minutes (or as long as you need) to reflect on what rose for you during this meditation. You might find it helpful to jot down any thoughts, questions or insights that came to mind.

Audio link for frisbee meditation
https://www.room478.com/frisbee-meditation/

***

Strength

Our minds are a doorway to the depths of our being.

Through this doorway we can build anything. The source of inner strength comes from our minds, and we can develop this strength by observing our thoughts and emotions. By becoming more mindful. Love sits within our heart and when that mind-heart connection is formed growth is inevitable.

We all have inner strength, willpower. By being compassionate towards ourselves our ability to deal with a situation is far better placed and we are stronger as a result.

People rehearse for shows, train for marathons and revise for tests. Why would you not spend some time on training your mind, so you know how to deal with what life may throw at you? Be equipped to manage situations as best you can when they arise.

Meditation is a great way to observe your thoughts, yourself and exercise your mind.

Strength will get you through the darkest of times. We have the strength within us, we just need to make time for our minds.

Staying open encourages growth. Growth helps you connect with your heart. That connection with your heart then makes staying open come more easily if we don't get distracted!

***

The opposite of distraction

The opposite of distraction is, wait for it, attraction. What we really need to do is increase our attraction. When we are attracted to something, we're naturally focused. We're naturally able to be present.

When I first I heard this, I thought, *No it's not ... Hang on, is it?*

It's played on my mind a lot since I first heard it, but I'm starting to get it.

Reading it time and time again, I began to understand how this is true: to be present – truly present – attracted to what we have, means we are indeed distracted, totally focused on the attraction. Away from all the outside noise. We're open.

We are so caught up in facts that we are told or taught, we sometimes don't even question if there is another possibility ... a different answer?

What thoughts come to your mind when you read this?

Feel it to Heal it

Laid beneath the surface, the smiles turn to fear,
Not brave enough to turn to or ask of anybody near.
Holding back emotion, trying to pull through,
Burying your voice and many parts of you.

Longing to find meaning, for it to go away,
The worry and panic they lead the mind astray.
Not wanting to feel sadness or facing what you have lost,
Parts of you now hidden, but with it comes a cost.

Emotion feels uncomfortable, yet in ways you then feel free,
Unexplainable to start with: this 'letting things just be'.
Why did I resist it, and bury all the pain,
When I lean into this feeling, there is so much to gain.

Removing expectation and other peoples' views,
I take my time and find my breath; I know what I must do.
Healing, it is possible, there is a pathway out,

Trust in what you're feeling, make room to simply shout.

Don't hide beneath the surface, there is so much more in view,
Feel what you feel, and take it slow; the healing lies in you.

***

Chapter 11

Feel it to Heal it

I SEEM TO have two modes: either full of creativity, ideas overflowing, like I can't wait to begin; or the alternative (which used to be the more frequently rising of the two) presenting with *oh my god ... this is shit ... I am shit ... I can't do it*. Even drafting this book, the imposter arrived, sitting on my shoulder with a whole speech prepared for me. Criticism prompts fear and the spiral begins. It takes over.

It took me quite some time to push through these walls which kept arising. I knew I was pushing down how I felt, not brave enough to share my fears, but still I kept writing. I began to soften and make peace with the privacy of my own thoughts and feelings, and started to see that each time I sat with how I felt, or wrote down what was simply present for me, the fear and self-doubt faded ever so slightly and as time went on this new habit of being with whatever was here really started to roll into more of what I was doing. Confident in simply being myself and sharing what I meant more often didn't feel so scary any more. I no longer wanted to hide it.

Sometimes we just need to feel the way we feel.

It is a basic need to feel seen, be heard and understood, that's not unreasonable. The thing is some people won't see you, nor hear what you are saying, and this is why it often takes a while to get comfortable with how you feel. Until one day you show up just as you are and the words that flow out of your mouth are captured in a way you haven't experienced before. It's why you need to find your people.

***

I HAVE HAD some hard lessons when it comes to finding people who truly see me. The me I want to be without having to fit in, being less or doing more. The places where I can just show up where I am not too much, too emotional. Then harder still is finding people who do fully see you, like no one ever has before, but then they slip away from you, leaving you heartbroken. Once more questioning if it would be better to try and fit in all over again. Yet I keep going, wanting to feel and find meaning. Catching the glimmers. Walking forward, heart wide open, knowing in this broken open heart lies more lessons. I feel I'm kicking and screaming in resistance to it, yet I know the deal! I must lean in! But it hurts! So bad! Still I remind myself once more: this is all part of it; what's truly meant for me won't pass me by, it just might not yet be the right time. Until the lesson is learnt the same situations will keep repeating themselves. So I buckle up, ready to listen this time, and get ready for the next sea of emotions.

Why does this happen? Some people remain in your life for a long time, though they are distant, mean and critical.

Others fleet through yet make a significant impact ... and then gone, just like that. Yes, this can cause damage, heartache and sadness, but does it mean we shouldn't feel it? Should we trying to cling to 'happiness' all the time instead?

Suppression of our feelings only builds and eventually the pressure becomes too much. At times, you may not even know how you are feeling until you have allowed yourself to express this.

Going through life is difficult; it is not easy; there is no straight path forward.

We must ask ourselves, why do we feel the way we do? What is it that we need? Why do we so often bury and suppress feeling that we should be able to (and more importantly *need*) to feel?

***

We are so often told not to cry, not to worry. The message engrained: not to welcome feeling anything less than happy.

I cry. A lot. And I know that this makes other people uncomfortable. My dad only allows his tears out at the sport or when watching a good band and even then, holding it back.

Uncontrollable laughter is viewed as something acceptable, and even beneficial, but an irrepressible flow of tears makes most people uncomfortable. Society teaches us that if we cry there is an issue, so then those around us think there is something to fix; another problem; something to be solved and that if we stop crying then there is no problem. But all it does is push it down, this emotion festering under the surface.

Conventionally, happy emotions are welcomed and therefore it's more comfortable to express feeling this way.

Crying is simply an expression of how we feel in that moment. So too is anger and all other emotions that we may not even understand, making it more difficult to acknowledge and accept where we are and how we feel. We should treat each emotion with the same respect and space: this is what makes way for us to heal. With the lack of the vocabulary to communicate exactly how we feel in any given moment, it can be helpful to have a visual image. Take a look at the wheel of emotions in the Mindful Moments section at the back of this book for some guidance.

Mindfulness teaches us to be aware of our feelings and accept them, whatever they are. This is the healthiest response and while it can be uncomfortable and painful at times, it's releasing something, freeing up space inside for the energy to flow more freely.

***

Happiness

ACCORDING TO THE Buddha, mindfulness is the source of happiness and joy.

The Buddha has a sutra on happiness, the Mangala Sutta. He says happiness is possible in the present moment: this is the only place you will find it as that is what is here, it's where you are. We all get caught up in finding happiness in things, what's to come and endless plans that we don't even see that we have everything already to feel this happiness in the present moment.

Don't let today pass you by waiting for tomorrow. Things will happen when the time is right. Enjoy today, smile more, notice happiness in what you have already, in what you see, in this moment, inside you.

We can't do everything at once and we can't be in more than one place at a time, we can only ever do things in this moment.

It's so beneficial to release this pressure from yourself. As someone who surrounded themselves in task after task with not a moment to spare, believe me when I say you get the same things done by slowing down and enjoying the moment rather than being overwhelmed by the upcoming to-dos.

I have spent vast amounts of time being overwhelmed by the future, things I had to do or just concerns and worries much of the time. It didn't get me anywhere any faster, it just caused high amounts of anxiety and stress, taking me away from enjoying today. I still get caught up in it sometimes but now I remind myself to take things one moment at a time.

When things seem too much, it is quite easy to get overwhelmed and if we don't bring ourselves back to the moment it just builds up.

When focused on one moment at a time it unfolds more naturally, with ease. The more moments you take one by one, the more you see and the less stress you live under.

Break it down: today is all you must think about.

***

WHAT DOES HAPPINESS mean to you? Are you always searching for it?

Realising that happiness isn't just going to show up when we arrive somewhere changed my outlook. Just like love, happiness is a way of living: your heart's path. It can be easy to take the small things, the treasures in simplicity for granted. I missed so many of these moments on my constant search outside myself. I often held on to the destination, or the event, the night out to bring this nicely wrapped gift of happiness on arrival. To find that unless I had a few more drinks I didn't feel quite as happy as in the vision in my mind.

People search for happiness in lots of external things but as with love, you need to find your happy in you. I've heard more than a few people say, 'I'll be happy when this is over.' Many people said this during lockdown but happiness arrived for me each day when I stopped; those were some of the most profound moments. Of course, we face challenge and difficulty, but happiness is not on hold. There will be times when life is hard, things won't go our way. Along the way we lose people, or find we're not in the life you once mapped out, but you're right where you are and that is where it all sits. I remember a while ago hearing an elderly lady in a shop saying to (I presume) her granddaughter, 'If you're always wanting more, dear, you will never have enough.' This is true enough in all walks of life: needing to appreciate more of the little things, the moment. We find ourselves right here. So much time spent lost in the ideal once more of what we think is the right thing, of what we should be doing.

Lockdown was a real wake-up call for me. Over nearly four years on, as I finalise this part of my story of discovery, I see that losing yourself happens so subtly over time you don't even notice. It is finding your way back that appears harder and seems to take a longer time, but this is more to do with the fact that on the discovery you are aware, you notice, you're mindful of it. When you lose yourself, it isn't as noticeable as much of it is wrapped in self-destruction and distraction, the time, the years just pass. (It's a little like trying to lose a few pounds after an all-inclusive holiday: a week goes by and you don't see the pounds piling on, but they quickly do if you allow it, then getting those pounds back off takes time.) Habits form and falling into them is easier than confronting them. During the months of Covid-19, the constant stream of news and sad stories meant any feeling happiness held an element of guilt, but why? Happiness is found in sharing a smile, reading a book, getting outside and for many this enforced time at home provided ample space to be happy, if our minds allowed it.

Experiencing happiness doesn't mean we don't care. The point I kept coming back to during journaling was that much of the sadness and fear felt inside me was because I felt that's what I should be doing. I lost myself for a while and felt guilty for enjoying a peaceful walk with my family, no traffic whizzing by. It just goes to show that if we place the outcome outside of ourselves and the moment, if we compare our lives to somebody else's, then once more we lose ourselves again.

There is a time and place for all emotions. Of course, we will all go through times where we are not always happy, but you don't automatically have to live in unhappiness as a situation changes: we all have the choice. As a way of controlling how we want to feel, we often end up blocking how we truly feel, which is often why you may turn up to a long-awaited night out and without a couple of bottles of wine inside you, you can't enjoy it all. Don't block the feelings that come to you. Get comfortable with them, because they're yours.

When stuck in the constant stream of needing to feel sad or scared because the news is saying so, or extremely happy now that you have been taken out somewhere or been bought a gift, a pattern forms and the emotions you may actually feel don't fit into the situation, so they are suppressed. You feel lost once more but scared to explain it. As time goes by, I see that self-discovery fosters happiness through healing. Connection to yourself and others strengthens in these spaces.

***

There is no way to happiness, happiness is the way. – **Thich Nhat Hanh**

I often remind myself of this quote. Happiness can be the way for you: you can find all the joy you desire inside yourself. By simply seeing and feeling happiness in our day-to-day lives this extends to everything else we view.

Whilst shopping this week I saw an elderly couple pushing their trolley, side by side. Slowly walking together, both holding the trolley handle. The elderly man leaned over to his wife (I assumed!), tapped her on the bum, gave her a little kiss on the cheek and on they went. The lady had a little giggle and continued smiling as they walked on. (I hope I still get a tap on the bum when I'm older!) This scene in front of me lit up my whole day, everything else I saw made me smile and I loved how this elderly couple were finding happiness on their way round the supermarket.

Emotion vs feeling

When we become aware of these feelings it can be difficult, emotional, especially if we have spent years suppressing them! I recently read 'We can suppress emotion, but we can't not feel.' As our feelings rise this is where we see emotion.

If we suppress emotion, we are walking around with these buried feelings. Those around us unaware of why we may be short-tempered, not bothered, distant, drinking too much, staying up late, not sleeping. The list goes on. Now, I'm not saying we spend all day crying, the next day smashing some plates up, releasing the anger, but the emotion needs space to present itself, at a time that's safe for you to do so and there are many things we can do to express, to safely feel the emotions present within us and when we do, healing happens.

My suggestions and things that help me are:

- Meditation.
- Breathwork.
- Group circles and open space, to be able to talk freely.
- Community and connection.
- Ecstatic dance.
- Cacao ceremony.
- Sound healing.

There is so much available out there and more I am not even aware of, I'm still exploring all the time but these few listed above really provide a space to connect with my emotions. I keep going back and it's helping. Not forgetting my all-time favourite thing to do when expressing emotion: writing! I seem to express in the form of poetry, this flows for me, and I've shared a few throughout this book.

Ultimately feel into what works for you and, when you can, let the emotion come.

***

Meditation: because some questions can't be answered by Google!

WE ALL REACH for the internet, our phones, laptops, constant newsfeeds, social media … online access to a wealth of answers at our fingertips. Whilst I am profoundly grateful to the resources available from this vault of information, when it comes to finding yourself, the answers you need are individual. We all travel differently so there won't be a one answer fits all available online.

Slowing down and listening, seeing what's here, feeling what's inside may all sound so simple but it's amazing once you do. We really do have the answers, they just need to be discovered. Meditation and self-inquiry helped me to do this, I am indebted to it. Beautiful things right in front of our eyes which we miss when clouded with doubt, fear and questions.

Finding yourself and following the correct path is so rewarding; mindfulness and meditation has been a doorway into this new way of life. Each day a new beginning, a chance for further growth. Whatever the day brings I can now see clearer. I'm constantly more aware, whatever the weather.

Try and explore being present for a moment, ask *yourself* a question you once might have tapped into Google for reassurance and see what comes to you.

I now choose carefully what I read, I don't watch the news, I spend more time watching what's in front of my eyes and let me tell you, there is so much peace and happiness there.

***

What we resist persists

By resisting we are still giving those thoughts power, therefore drawing them to our minds.

It was renowned Swiss psychiatrist Carl Jung who taught us that whatever you resist persists. What he meant by that is the more you resist anything in life, the more you bring it to you.

This is so true, resistance absorbs so much time; resistance to something still holds a place in your thoughts. You try putting it off or removing it all together, whatever it may be for you, in turn we inadvertently give it power, it then persists! A simple example: you want a piece of chocolate (surely we've all had this desire?) but you think, *I can't, I shouldn't, I won't.* All this time what's at the forefront of your mind? The chocolate!

The opposite of resisting is to embrace and confront it, allow it to be (of course this goes deeper than the chocolate). If we do this it will move through more naturally without holding persistent attention. This isn't always easy especially with things we don't like, at work, household chores, painful memories, yet just like with our anxious thoughts, if we stop forcing them to leave, they will naturally move on. We all must face and do things that aren't pleasant: resistance to these things allows us to be consumed by it. Having acceptance and living in the moment, being with what is here, not resisting – allow it to be and it will pass through easier. Denial is a temporary fix; those underlying forces always surface.

Simply acknowledging takes some of the resistance away: in time whatever you are resisting will become easier. Resistance is a psychological reaction to change, it's often the change that we fight, not necessarily the task in hand. You don't need to tell yourself you can't have it, or that you must resist it. Start by seeing why you chose not to have it or don't want to face it yet. Acknowledge how you feel and allow these feelings.

Living mindfully, aware of feelings and thoughts rather than allowing them to take over does free your mind. You're not resisting anything – you are noticing what is, without judgement.

See if you can allow something today to be as it is, get on with it, sit with it, don't resist it – whatever it is that comes up for you, in turn it should resolve quicker and not persist.

Love persists anyway, love holds strong.

If the future seems overwhelming, remember that it comes one moment at a time. – **Beth Mende Conny**

***

YESTERDAY IS HISTORY, **tomorrow is a mystery, but today is a gift. That is why we call it the present.** Each time I read this (the quote attributed to many individuals) gratitude floods me once more and I smile at being here today. That I'm alive, that I can now connect more with the present.

Being able to be truly present in today is indeed a gift. Mindfulness enables you to be fully present so you can appreciate and enjoy everything you already have. Everything you feel, everything you are.

If we are too busy, we don't have time to see and feel the beauty inside of us and all of life in front of us. I now see by living more presently that I was mostly living in the future, always in what's to come, what to do next. My anxiety was a coping mechanism to escape facing my fears, the hurt and the pain. Living this way, I was missing much of the joy in this moment. This is where anxiety takes us: forwards to try and control outcomes, fearing what's ahead. When constantly stuck in regret of wishing things had been done differently, we are going back. Depression rises when kept in this place for too long.

We can all get held up momentarily in what we should have done, but we can release the regret of the past, free this and let go. The same applies to the future: don't allow yourself to get caught up in endless lists, the fears and anxiety of what's yet to come – it is just time spent wasted as you do not know what's to come anyway; it is always going to be a mystery as it hasn't happened yet. This reminds me once more the importance of welcoming the feelings but letting them go. To connect with the pause once more. The inhale showing us where you've been, pausing in the present moment and then exhaling forwards.

PAUSE – Enjoy the gift you have right now, here in today.

***

Happiness is a state of inner fulfilment

SOMETIMES YOU CAN search a lifetime for happiness in external things. You will of course have happy times in new places and feel happy when you receive or experience new things. But to find true happiness and fulfilment you must look within.

We find happiness in what we notice, what we see. In the present moment. First you notice the happiness, then you feel it.

You will assume happiness is when you eat something you enjoy, surround yourself with people you love or go on holiday somewhere nice, but that isn't the happiness as such – it's the noticing. If you were busy reading a book while eating something lovely you may not notice the food; in turn you don't get the happiness from it. Instead, the happiness may be in the book as that's where your attention is. The same is true for recognising the happiness within you – notice it, feel it. That is the happiness.

You need to see and appreciate what you already have. See this in you and in others. It will not come from the things you don't yet have – they are not here.

Appreciate you, your kindness, your ability to listen and love, plus many more. We can still feel happiness even if the outside seems a bit rocky at times.

Notice your happiness today – it is there.

Who doesn't like feeling happy? We really do have all the basic equipment we need to achieve the happiness we want. We can resurface memories that make us smile and yet still be present with the feelings felt.

Start with you! You have it all there inside, it really is the best place to start. It may sometimes be hard to find but you will find it – and once you do, everything you see will be beautiful.

You truly can find happiness within yourself, so look no further.

***

The sun is always shining

Sometimes we don't always see the sun or feel its brightness, but it is still shining.

This applies to so many things, like the news. There is still good news to be read, good things happening each day, we just don't always see it. Every opening webpage, pop-up or newspaper may have something concerning, worrying, or upsetting at the front – it can feel overwhelming. Reading or hearing too much of anything, putting too much focus on it just blows things up in your mind.

When learning how to manage my anxiety around health the most helpful thing I learnt is that I am in control. Just because I don't want to read or hear all the bad news, or see or speak to a friend, doesn't mean I don't care. We can easily get overwhelmed by what we think we should be doing; by fear. It's not nice or fair on us to go through it constantly, especially when we don't need to. Of course, there will be times we all feel scared, or sad, or a little worried but we don't want to live each day like this, do we? We can save these emotions for when we need them. We can't or shouldn't feel bad and worry every day for everyone.

***

Share a smile

THE POWER OF a single smile is amazing: it could transform someone's day. Smiling is also contagious, so share your smile with as many people as you see.

Have you ever been walking down the street, feeling a bit down, then somebody looks over at you and gives you a big warm smile? When you feel that smile it's very difficult for it not to rub off on you.

Feel the change in yourself as you smile – do it right now and feel the difference.

Try taking a moment – now, if you can – take a pause. Take three deep mindful breaths. On the third exhalation say these affirmations to yourself:

- I am happy, I am smiling.
- I smile and I feel good.

- I smile often.
- I am grateful for what I have.
- I am grateful for my smile.
- I smile and the world smiles back at me.
- I touch others with a soft, kind smile.
- I smile at life and in return life smiles at me.
- I see the best in everything and everyone.

(Repeat as many times as you want to.)

Through the simple act of smiling, we can solve problems, connect with others, feel happiness, and see the beauty in life in front of us.

In the wise words of Thich Nhat Hanh; 'Sometimes your joy is the source of your smile, but sometimes your smile can be the source of your joy.'

And even if today is not a great day – perhaps reading this invokes feelings of frustration – notice that and smile anyway. See what comes up for you: you might surprise yourself!

An extra challenge: try smiling and being angry at the same time … it's harder than you think!

***

THE BENEFITS OF smiling are plentiful. Smiling helps our bodies release cortisol and endorphins, fighting off stress and lowering blood pressure. Smiling even helps decrease pain and can strengthen our immune system! Various studies on smiling list endless benefits, one of which is that it may even increase your lifespan! Endorphins produced by smiling results in positive emotions. Another chemical released from the brain when you smile is serotonin, which is a natural antidepressant.

Smiling – your hidden superpower!

***

WE DON'T WANT to practise unhappiness. You don't hear anyone saying, 'I'm just waiting for this so I can be unhappy.' We must lift our spirits and make happiness our way. Smile, watch something that makes you laugh: give yourself permission to feel happiness. Listen to a great song, speak to a good friend, someone that lifts you up. Watch and spend time with your children as they grow. Enjoy a lovely walk, learn a new skill – feeling happiness doesn't have to be big. Take each day, each hour, each moment one step at a time.

But if you don't feel happy, that's ok too. I share a lot about the acceptance of *all* emotions. The point is, this is your experience on this earth, you can feel however you feel and that's ok.

What's more important is ensuring you don't compare yourself to others. Remove expectations and find your experience. This is the time you have power over. What's done is done. If you're reading this, I believe you must be on the pathway now to finding yourself. Are you ready to lean in? To feel into what is rising rather than resisting what is desperate to emerge? Those times when you were lost, now become lessons to pave your way forward. Keep going. There is so much negativity and hate out there. If we allow it in, we are lost once more. We all have choice and the best you can, choose you. Make space to feel what enters your heart and listen to this. Sometimes you just need to forget everyone and everything else and just be! And when you feel love, that warm, real, exciting, inexorable, complete feeling just grab hold of it. Through love comes healing. Feel into it!

***

Have a good cry, wash your heart out. If you keep it inside, it will tear you apart. – **Unknown**

HOLDING ON TO emotion, pain, fear, the past only delays healing. We frequently hold on to these things, we hold grudges. Keeping hold of such emotion only causes us pain, and if not processed or released it can indeed tear us apart.

I've read before that tears water the seeds of our growth. I love this way of looking at it – my future must be well watered! Potentially drowning! Some people cry more than others or may feel more comfortable doing so, others may not need to cry as much. The important thing is first to notice what you feel, then feel free to release your emotions. For whom are we keeping them in for?

It is so beneficial to face our difficulties, acknowledge whatever those feelings are and not push them away. This can take time and be hard to do but releasing pent-up emotion, being honest with yourself and what arises, allowing it to be there and sit just as it is – this is ok.

It is ok to cry, it's not a weakness. Water the seeds of your growth so you can move forward and flourish without anything weighing you down.

It can be a long process but by releasing these emotions at a pace that works for you, you will clear the way back to yourself so you can feel fully at home. Sometimes you may cry for no reason at all – just allow yourself to be and accept each moment for what it is. You likely wouldn't hold back a giggle, so give your tears the same grace.

At times nothing is required at all, the simple act of just not pushing away how you feel is all you need. Just mindful of however you're feeling. Comfortable in your own skin.

***

Do you try and push away bad and uncomfortable feelings?

When good things are happening to us, we naturally want to stay with that joy and feel every part of it. We embrace those happy feelings and living in that moment is much easier.

When we have bad feelings or go through a tough time we automatically try and shut it down. Sometimes going into this autopilot way of thinking just makes these challenging times even harder.

Sitting with the uncomfortable thoughts and feelings as well as the good is a healthy way to process these more challenging times and let them pass by naturally.

Try and explore something uncomfortable today and just notice what comes up. Observing your thoughts rather than being the thoughts.

Whether you're having a challenging day or a good day, just take a few minutes for yourself and take a breath. More importantly, notice those breaths you take today.

***

THE MORE HONEST and open you are, the less fear you will have.

Being honest can be hard, being open can be difficult. These things are often only a challenge to us because we put pressures and judgements on ourselves, these causing fears and anxiety.

Once we find who we are, when we are completely comfortable in our own skin and honest with ourselves the easier it is to be honest with others.

When you know who you are it's so freeing, all else outside of this can no longer take hold the way it once has before. Instead of resisting, you no longer need to worry about revealing your emotions. They are part of who you are.

Be honest and open and live a fulfilling life.

***

ONE OF THE reasons we can't find that place where things

become impossible is because it has become hidden underneath layers of fear and self-doubt. I recently read *The Subtle Art of not Giving a Fuck* by Mark Manson. (One of my recommended reads if you haven't read already, it's a book about hope.) In the book he compares self-awareness to an onion and how peeling these layers back is likely to induce crying when you least expect it!

When I read this, it really made me think about self-awareness and how important it is to open up to who we are, however difficult this sometimes may be. When we peel back the layers and access what's inside we can be free; we can feel what's present; we can heal. Reading Mark Manson's onion analogy inspired me to write a meditation for a group I was leading, and I share this with you here. Create a quiet moment and explore this now. (If you prefer to listen to meditations, I have provided an audio recording for this; you'll find the link below.)

***

Onion meditation

I WANT YOU to take a moment now, just connect with yourself, connect with the seat. Your feet firmly on the ground. Take a nice deep breath in, stretching up your spine … as you slowly exhale just allow your shoulders to soften. Really find your connection. Find your breath, your rhythm.

So, deepening your breathing now, become aware of where your breath feels most comfortable for you.

Notice how you feel as you become aware of your breathing. We are going to try and adopt an openness as we expand our self-awareness.

Imagine an onion, with this onion in mind, I want us to move through this meditation thinking about peeling back our own layers. There is no pressure; no right or wrong way.

The thought of this may feel uncomfortable, or it may feel inviting, but whatever thoughts and feelings arise for you right now just allow yourself to explore them, peeling back the layers to who you are and to what you feel.

All we are doing is being open and present as we sit for this meditation.

Now bring your attention to your eyes … if they're closed just feel the comfort of them closed. If they're open just allow your gaze to either soften or close your eyes completely.

Your breath flowing through your body, your shoulders relaxed.

Take note of what comes to the forefront of your mind when you think of what 'space' means to you.

Taking the next few moments to pause, to reflect.

We are going to try and create a little space for you to gently unfold the layers within you.

Firstly, spend a little time thinking about the layers that

you build up around yourself: habits, pressures, things you think you must do. Ways in which you think you must be and things you so often suppress …

As you think about this, just do so with care. If anything arises that's overwhelming, just allow it to be as it is – even if just for a moment. Allow yourself to feel the way that you feel. At any time, you can always guide yourself back to your breath.

Taking the next few moments to pause, to explore.

Sometimes things happen, feelings arise, and we face situations – some we may not be prepared for. We may not understand the meaning or we may try and resist what we truly feel or what we want to do, all the while suppressing more and more.

We suppress things for fear of judgement, for fear of losing things or sometimes simply just not being ready for changes.

Give yourself permission to take this time to think about the layers built up around you.

Take the next few moments to pause, to feel.

Whatever comes into your mind right now just allow it to be there; let yourself ease into any feelings that arise. Allow your feelings about these thoughts to be exactly as they are and allow your emotions to be just as they are; simply notice where you feel this in your body.

Now on your next breath in, peel back the first layer to you – to what you need.

Take a moment now to think about how you are feeling and what you are uncovering.

Use the next few moments to pause, to feel.

Connect with your breathing once more, noticing the gentle rise and fall in your body; your own rhythm of breath. If this isn't noticeable for you, that's ok, just gently place your hand on your abdomen as you allow your breath to come and go in its natural flow.

Bring your awareness to the second layer now as you connect a little deeper with yourself.

Again, just notice what arises for you at this time.

Bring a little curiosity to these thoughts and feelings that come up for you. Lean into any feelings or sensations in your body; just once again note what you uncover as you peel back this layer.

If no thoughts are present at this time, this is ok too; just come back to your breath, bringing awareness to the rise and fall within.

Take the next few moments to pause, to heal.

And now come back to your breath: the gentle inhale, the soft exhale. Simply notice how you feel. Allow any emotions to present as we move through to peel back the third layer.

As you think about peeling back this layer, allow the question 'why' to arise: ask yourself why you feel the way you do, knowing that whatever comes up for you here is ok.

Be present with yourself in this moment. Just allow the exploration to arise: whatever comes up for you is relevant and allow it to be just as it is, there is no need to change anything.

Explore this place inside where everything is possible.

You can peel back as many layers as you feel comfortable for you. If you just want to sit with one layer that's completely fine … Just give yourself a moment to explore the way that you're feeling, observe what emotions may be present.

As you continue to explore, keep taking your time, as much time as you need, feel free to remain seated with your eyes closed and allow your awareness to expand …

When you're ready, gently starting to notice your breath again. As you inhale and exhale allow yourself to feel the connection with your seat. Notice any sounds in the room around you, any sounds outside. Feel the temperature in the room.

Gently wriggle your toes, use gentle movement in your shoulders, and as you slowly bring your awareness to the room around you, I want you to think of a tree.

A tree strips back its layers every year and even with its bare branches – its beauty still present.

Take a final deep breath in now and, if you haven't already done so, as you exhale just gently open your eyes.

Take a moment to journal on what has risen and remember: be gentle and compassionate with yourself.

Audio link for onion meditation:
https://www.room478.com/onion-meditation/

***

Empathy

I DIDN'T REALLY understand what empathy was for a long while, confused by its meaning for a long time. I have always been told that I am too sensitive, to pull myself together, the tears too much sometimes. All this making me a little self-conscious, as easily feeling emotion was depicted as a negative.

It wasn't until somebody referred to me as an Empath (with no negative connotations) that I decided I wanted to fully understand the meaning of it. Not only do I now understand and appreciate this quality, I embrace it; I am grateful for it.

Empathy is the ability to sense other people's emotions and really feel them.

You can imagine and understand just how someone else feels in a situation. It goes beyond hearing – you register and feel the information on a deep level from people around you, within the room. It just happens. You can even sense their feelings by just being there, understanding exactly what they may need. Sometimes you know what people want before they even ask for it or express it.

While empathy is wonderful, it can sometimes be too much. If you can feel other people's feelings on a magnified level or someone becomes dependent on your empathy it can drain your own resources, meaning you can burn out quickly as you are enduring all these different feelings as well as your own. When someone is sad or feeling low, I feel it deep inside. I cry for someone else's sadness as well as my own.

It's good to understand and care about how others feel. It helps us connect with people and care for them, as we reach out when they need help, rather than when they simply ask for it. Understanding and feeling the way somebody else feels can be extraordinary, but it's important to find a balance so you also look after yourself. It's ok to need distance when this gets too much. This can be hard at times as you really take on and feel another person's emotions and views. As a reiki practitioner I understand the importance of clearing energy, so if you take other people's energy in remember this too. (See the guide at the back of the book for some tips on how to clear energy.)

I love to help, love, surprise and look after people, of course, but it is important that with this we find balance and compassion for ourselves too.

Make sure you find the balance that works for you but be sure to embrace who you are, not hide it.

Let it hurt, let it heal, let it go ...

LET IT HURT. A valuable lesson I have learnt is that it's ok to sit with pain, unwanted feelings, discomfort, even heartbreak. All too often we are quick to push away feelings we don't want. This behaviour is natural but this action actually gives the feelings more attention, making the hurt last longer. Of course, it's not pleasant sitting with some of this but it helps us heal. Good feelings come and go with ease because we are happy to sit with them, enjoy them for what they are and allow them to pass. But when I feel anxious, I start to worry, I don't want to sit with it at all, so I focus on pushing the worry away. The worry then gets bigger and bigger ... Letting things hurt enables you to process; from this you make progress.

Let it heal. Giving yourself space and time, you are allowing yourself to heal. You cut your knee? You would clean it, air it, cover it with a plaster, then let it heal. The same applies to your mind. Give yourself space, be kind to yourself, feel what you feel and make time for the care and comfort you need to heal.

Let it go. This, for me, is the hardest part but like all of us I'm learning every day! Holding on is hurting nobody but yourself. I have caused myself a lot of hurt when holding on to unwanted and unnecessary things, grudges, feelings. When you finally do get to the point where you can let go, you are free. Absolutely free, untouchable! It's quite amazing really.

If you find this hard, start with something small. Remember, before you heal you must let it hurt. Then you can let it go.

***

If the ocean can calm itself, so can you. We are both salt water mixed with air. – **Nayyirah Waheed**

EACH OF US experiences our own challenges. Whatever that may be for you, it is important to know that amongst all the chaos, panic, change, different views and high emotions there will always come a place of calm.

You can find your own calm inside; you can transition to a different state of mind and move forward, despite change. Although the world may not be as you know it right now, and highs and lows may surface like the crashing waves on the shore, deep down at the bottom of the water, although we cannot see it, the waves are calm, peaceful, beautiful.

You may need to leave some things, places and even people behind in order to find your calm and that's ok. Shift your focus and use your wisdom to transition forward. You will still be there when you find it. Everything else is just stuff! It's all about the simple things. Find your breath, find your calm.

Take time to explore beneath the surface, then in time, allow all your parts of you to be seen. In making time and creating space to feel how you feel, the healing takes place.

You too can calm yourself – just like the ocean

***

Love Your Story

Love your story, embrace it all,
The pain, the laughter, and the falls.
Each step worthy, holding space,
The unique tale, yours to embrace.

Tears they fell and felt so deep,
The memories are now yours to keep.
Lessons learnt and love unfolds,
Each step closer to make you whole.

Adventure, friendship, that special kiss,
Moments which are not to be missed.
Romance, loss and trauma comes,
Emotion rises like the sun.

Feel it, see it, don't shut it down,
For each experience moves your world around,
To where you are, stood here today,
This story, yours, so have your say.

***

Chapter 12

Love Your Story

AND SO IT is! I decided to love my story, no longer thinking I'm not good enough. Time and time again comparison held me back. I'd almost get there and then hear of someone else doing something similar. Inferiority taking hold once more, my own light dimming. Something inside me never gave up. Despite that voice at times still rising, it never stopped me being drawn into more and more supportive and open spaces to brighten my sparkle and strengthen my belief.

***

Love

I INVITE YOU to question once more: what is love anyway?

Love has so many meanings, differently felt within us all. Multiple thoughts behind this one word. The feeling of love, being in love, loving another, loving you.

But only when you show love and kindness to yourself can you then share this with others on a deeper level.

It comes back to love in all moments in some way, shape or form – people, places, food, animals, books, music. Even in the sad times love is present.

Love really is all around. We give love, feel love, see love, hear love – we are love. We are all connected.

Love has so many meanings. Each person defines love in their own way, but we all feel it and, like anything, the more you are able to feel love within, feeling love for yourself, the more the feelings grow. When you feel it inside, the more it oozes out of you too.

What does love to mean to you?

***

LOVE WHAT YOU see, see what you love.

It really can be this simple. You will see more of what you love if you love what you see; this includes you. Pay attention to the things you love. The more you notice a connection to love each day, the more it will begin to stand out. This could be from the love for yourself or simply from doing things you love. Before you know it, you are surrounded by love. You'll be in a bubble of love!

What a wonderful place to be. Who doesn't want to feel loved, give love and see love everywhere?

This applies to us, too. Love what you see in yourself. Whichever emotions we nurture, they grow. If we give ourselves the right environment we shall blossom. Don't allow people to put you down and burst your bubble. You are in control of you, you deserve all the love you feel.

Love is all around us, just expand your awareness. You will begin to see and feel it everywhere. Giving love is wonderful and so important but we must remember to let it come back in too.

It all comes back to love.

***

Take a moment and look in the mirror, look yourself right in the eye and say, 'I love you!' Simply notice, is it easy? Was there resistance? Did it flow? Did it feel easy, comfortable? The experience is yours and you can affirm whatever you like here. But best you can, remember to love your story …

Love you

Love you enough that you give yourself care,
Love you so much you don't mind if they stare.
Love you completely and set yourself free,
Love you and your needs so you can just be.
Love you for lifting my mood when I'm down,
Love you for giving me strength not to drown.
Love you for hearing despite there no sound.
Love you for helping me talk myself round.

Love you each day over, again and again,
Love you forever and you shall not end.
Love you.

***

Nothing helps you learn about emotions and feelings like heartache. A multitude of lessons wrapped up in the pain. It's inevitable: opposites meet, and we find resolution, but we have to feel it all to grow. When sat deep in the pain, I question love; I've done so many a time, but I conclude that I do agree with the quote 'it's better to have loved and lost, than to never have loved at all.'

A moment, an hour, a year, a decade – previous moments. We can search a lifetime, making mistakes along the way, holding on, not letting go. Doing the right thing but by who? But then, suddenly out of nowhere, it catches you. 'Nothing more than this.' Than what? Than love – it doesn't matter where or how you find it, but do you notice it? The greatest love just hits you like a bolt out of nowhere; not looking for it, but it's there, it's deep and there is no denying what you feel. The only problem can be timing: moments of love and happiness can so easily pass you by if you're still stuck in your head, rather than allowing such moments to flow freely. Until both souls start from this point, this perfect understanding of two souls will remain on hold.

Love is what it all comes back to, so when you feel it slipping away that cuts deep. Something you thought would never fade no longer sits as it once was, but it doesn't mean you should cling on. Change happens to us all, we lose people and gain others all the time, moving forward in the concept of time, inevitably, ageing takes place and before you know it everything looks different.

The problem is sometimes we lose ourselves in somebody else's vision, getting diverted from our own path. It's good to compromise but when you no longer have anything left, all imprints of you faded, a time comes when recognition of your life doesn't feel familiar. It creeps up, placing so much focus on what we haven't got. When you start to see what you have got, when you begin to see you, you rise back up, but this can be a challenge. Those around you, used to the way you were and your growth unrecognised can make you feel lost once more.

If you come back to love, that calling mountain, the heart's path often takes over. Doubt may rise, but trust it.

***

I'VE NEVER BEEN afraid of love. Despite inner turmoil I keep going back for more and if I feel it, I'm not afraid to say it. Reminded always of the scene in *My Best Friend's Wedding*, where they move under the bridge on the boat and he looks at her; that moment where we are reminded how moments and time pass us by. The importance of expressing how you feel: if you feel it just say it! All my life I've said it, I've captured the moment, even before the understanding of mindfulness was in my orbit. I've said those three words, then stood in the silence, not hearing them said back. Yet I've dived in again anyway.

Some may say brave, others may say stupid, but to me I felt it and it's one thing that didn't sit on the pile of unspoken words.

Life is hard. It's a real challenge to listen to your heart, but it doesn't fail you.

I've always clung on to an ideal of love, the longing for somebody to sweep me off my feet. It's hard: the movies show us many examples of this perfection, social media filled with what appears to be the perfect love, and around us couples seem to be free from drama, and instead candlelit dinners, endless time. The thing is we see what we want much of the time. Have you longed for a baby and seen many pregnant women? Just bought a new car and then see multiples of the exact car you now sit in? We attract what we put out there so if wishing to be loved in your ideal way is always at the forefront of your mind, you will see these perfect scenarios popping up in front of you, over and over. The longing to fit in, appear perfect in somebody's eyes, you're not alone. It took me a long time to see, that in this 'longing' lies the problem. Yes, for so long I didn't see it. (And to be clear I still love that kind of love, being loved in a way that makes your heart flutter.) I wanted a fluffy kind of love, an overwhelming feeling of lust and longing – all the time. Yet I always desired unavailable people in some way. I was looking for something that didn't exist. Something that only existed inside me. I couldn't see what I was doing for a long time.

Now, I'm able to question *why* I still cling to this ideal of love; to observe the feelings that come up rather than becoming attached to the outcome or goal set in my mind. I'm not saying that there isn't a love that knocks you sideways and that special someone out there, there is. I've felt it. The problem is you will keep meeting challenge after challenge until you fully see yourself. I see now that all the blocks that got in the way of me receiving this sort of love came from me. Love all of who you are and realise that you are enough, because until you do, nobody else will be fully available to you. And in that moment – as hard as it is – sometimes you just have to walk away.

***

RECENTLY I WAS teaching at a couples retreat and there was a speaker there holding a workshop. I was sat there on my own as I was also teaching but got to sit in on this workshop. A question was posed to the couples. To one of the ladies, 'How do you see men?' 'Difficult,' she answered. The same question to one of the men, 'How do you see women?' 'Caring,' he said. The relationship coach proceeded to discuss how we view people in our relationships. So, for example, the relationship I have with women may be reflective on my relationship with my mum. The same with the relationships I have with men, influencing how I perceive my dad, brother etc.

Always journal in hand, I noted some thoughts and again uncovered tiny threads back to myself once more. My exploration of self-discovery has not ended. It never will. But this ongoing journey includes and incorporates the most worthwhile steps I've taken. **I invite you to do the same.**

I feel that everyone has a limit. Each limit will of course be different, but they are there. Exactly when that lid will burst off is unknown, just as anything is. But when we take on too much, when we don't slow down, take time or recharge, that explosion becomes more inevitable.

***

MORE RECENTLY – midway through my own final edit, ahead of sending this very book off – I attended a festival and again saw someone else who had written a book of poems. *Oh no!* was my immediate thought, *Mine are useless.* Then the message rose again for what would be the fifth time now. This book isn't about me, it's about sharing what has come to me, what has been brought to my life in order to help others brighten their own light too. To live their life fully and understand that this world needs all of us, every single one. We all have our own gifts and the more this message is shared, the more people will hear it.

Love your story, the chapters already written and pages yet to come. Those pages you choose to write, decide how long those chapters are. Each part of your own unique story has brought you to this moment: you have already learnt so much and taught so many, you just may not realise it yet.

If something comes to you, trust it. If that feeling is so strong that you can't ignore it, listen. In loving fiercely – despite the fear – and relaxing a little, the creative flow will carry you forward.

I made a promise to myself that same morning – the

morning I watched someone else shine their light –not to dim my own light again. A bolt of light hit my soul and I knew in that moment that I not only wanted to but had to share my story and love each part of it too.

I decided to get really clear and stop being my biggest critic and cut myself a break. We all have fears and that niggling voice trying to take centre stage, knocking that signpost to a different path.

We learn when we teach, we teach when we learn and in the darkest time my pen has always held the candle, flickering when all the lights go out. At times, no sense is made of the words I see but they are strengthening my voice every time.

Now I'm allowing the golden space, the space to show up and share what I love.

***

There can't be a we until there's a me!

FINALLY, BEING ABLE to be present for the first time in so long, I stretched out, feeling the comfort of my sheets beneath me, the duvet cuddled round my body. I knew I had other things to do that day but for the first time in an awfully long time I was happy to stay put. I'd learnt to not rush every part of my day and it totally transformed who I was. I enjoyed my own company!

I still knew there were deadlines and start times, but finally, after years of anxiety and living at high speed yet running on empty, I knew I didn't have to any more. What a relief, to wake up and give myself a moment; not to be scared; free from panic; nor rely on being surrounded by noise and distraction, or people.

It was a grey morning outside; the air was calm, and I could hear my children in the next room discussing the tales of Harry Potter again! Many days the girls transformed their lives into this magical world and created their own adventures. Fantasising about the magic and creating amazing visions and tales following on from the books they'd read. *Why as an adult should it be any different?* I thought. Yes, of course responsibilities, work and commitments are present for us all, but we too can create our own magic! Or does that sound too easy? I began to see something that to many may seem so simple. Is this something that already comes with ease for you, or is it something you've not even yet considered?

I didn't need to give energy to anything outside this moment – I needn't get caught up ahead. Why had I spent years worrying about so much that hadn't even happened yet? I could say I wasted time, but I do feel that I learnt some valuable lessons bringing me to this point. I could enjoy

```
that lie-in! Enjoy those comfy bedsheets,
really enjoy the daily chaos of life which
is exactly what makes it perfect. The magic
right before my eyes - all along. I just
needed to find myself to appreciate it all.
My daughter diving on the bed, we giggled.
Not rushing for the next planned event. We
had a moment, felt connected, loved! And
that's what it's all about.
```

The anger I once held, the emotional let-down of past issues sometimes shaped my whole day ahead. My own trauma affected relationships. Waking up and knowing who I really was – I mean *really* knowing –changed my view on life.

I was still waking up in the same bed but instead of feeling overwhelmed and bogged down I felt great, great! It took the whole world to stop, literally, for me to get here but I'd made it! I'd found myself, after thirty-five years, two children and many ups and downs, I realised I was enough just as I was. Nobody else was me and I didn't need to be the same as anybody else.

Life has some wonderful moments if we allow ourselves to experience them. It is all made up of the little moments I'd once stressed over. I still experience stress and anger, but I don't become it. I don't feed it so that it snowballs out of control and takes over hours of my day. Days of my week! Weeks of the year!

***

'You will be faced with something from your past which you will have to deal with. This so crucial for your growth.' (A message on my tarot card, pulled from the deck that morning.)

What could it be? I thought. I began questioning the struggles at home, in my relationship, friendships, work … the list went on.

Then, there it was. December 2021: Christmas Day. Mum had a breakdown; she hadn't had one like this for a very long time. All emotions flushing forward. First, I wanted to fix it, then bury it, then I finally opened to allowing all the emotions to flow forward, past and present. What I didn't realise was these were the additional steps I needed to take to really come home to me.

***

I had written parts of this book but when I explored publishing it, something held me back. What I didn't know at the time was that it wasn't yet finished. Will it ever be? For after all, where are we trying to get to? Who is it that we want to be? Everyone in their own way is searching, but for what? To have the biggest house … hold the biggest parties … to have the most friends. To follow and be part of a group or religion. To have a family. These tend to crop up as the most common goals we assume we must strive for, but we don't have to: we find freedom in our own unique search.

On the outside things may appear fine but quite often everybody is struggling with something they'd rather not bring to the surface.

***

Because you are alive everything is possible. – **Thich Nhat Hanh**

TOO OFTEN DOUBT and judgement creep in, preventing us from being all that we can be. I have realised that most of the things I have felt not possible I prevented, through what I told myself. Many times, it was easier to list reasons why I can't or shouldn't, as that was often easier to believe – in turn making this my reality.

I find much meaning in this Thich Nhat Hanh quote: endless possibilities do await us all. By believing in ourselves and staying positive, we can achieve the once unthinkable if determined to do so.

Dare to let yourself dream the impossible today. Don't let limitations hold you back. You may need to take a different path to make your dreams come alive, but you can get there: remember to lean in and stay open.

Have the confidence in you and make it happen, you can make it possible.

Nothing is impossible, the word itself says I'm possible. – **Audrey Hepburn.**

***

ANXIETY IS NOT who I am but I'm grateful for it as without it I may have walked through the rest of my life racing ahead with my eyes closed. I wouldn't have met some of the amazing people who are now in my life, and I wouldn't be writing this, in the hope that it gives somebody else hope too. It has helped shape me, it has helped me find me and it has given me the passion to want to help others overcome this difficult road.

One of the most important things you can accomplish is just being yourself. – **Dwayne Johnson**

This truly is one of the most important things I have learnt and discovered over the past few years. It's quite draining busying yourself and constantly looking after everything around you just to avoid somethings you'd rather not face (for me, my anxiety). To be yourself, comfortable in your own skin, not hiding or pretending to anyone else – that is the answer. If you find the pretending outweighs the being, then it's not the place for you.

When you are true to you, so much weight is lifted. You can live happily, freely without the added pressure of being someone else.

Being yourself enables you to have better friendships and relationships with others, too. The bonds are more fulfilling and enjoyable, more truthful.

People will always judge us anyway whoever we may be, so we may as well at least be comfortable being who we are.

We spend all our time with ourselves so this relationship needs to be the most consistent, the most important.

Just as we try with others, our friends, our family, our children – we must do the same with ourselves. Ask yourself what you need, be kind to yourself, give yourself some care and compassion. Some time out, get to know who you are and what you really like.

Once you establish this relationship with you, everything around you becomes easier. We can be so hard on ourselves, our toughest critic, we judge ourselves and don't give ourselves a break. Change this, allow yourself what you need, make friends with yourself and accomplish being you.

You are the best friend you'll ever have.
Just let yourself in.

***

Love and forgiveness

WHEN YOU LOVE someone, you see all of them: the flaws and mistakes, plus all the wonderful qualities they have. We all have habits and traits, some that may annoy others or even unintentionally hurt them. Hence why forgiveness is so important. By not forgiving we mostly hurt ourselves.

Someone close to me shared Peter Ustinov's well-known quote 'love is an act of endless forgiveness, a tender look which becomes a habit.' I see that love is indeed endless moments of forgiveness, but this includes forgiveness of self.

To truly feel love you must start forgiving yourself, otherwise you reject the love you receive without even noticing.

In the past, I've held on to hurt and pain, not being able to forgive. Trust issues, feeling let down all part of this need to keep a guard up to protect myself. The thing is, this just stops us living, unless we forgive, let go and move on; then we can experience freedom and clearer thoughts. This doesn't mean you have to continue with people or things that make you unhappy or hurt you but for your own good try to forgive and move past it.

The biggest wake-up call is when you realise the first step is to apply this to yourself. You must love yourself for you to be able to feel love fully. To do this there will be times you need to forgive yourself again and again – this has not come easily to me, but it's so important. Forgiving yourself shows love and compassion and enables you to move forward. Forgive yourself, let go of what you've been holding on to or what you thought you should have done differently. Everything you've been through until now is part of your unique journey; it's brought you to today.

This applies to us all. Have you been holding on to something that you need to forgive yourself for? Have you loved someone who hasn't forgiven themselves either, in turn they don't let you in fully?

Show yourself some love and forgiveness today and every

day and encourage others to do the same.

Allow yourself to walk the path of healing.

Freedom and forgiveness

FREEDOM COMES FROM forgiveness.

To forgive is to set a prisoner free and discover that the prisoner was you. – **Lewis B. Smedes**

Holding on to unwanted feelings of anger and hatred keeps them alive inside us; in turn we then see many things in a negative way. This took me a long time not only to learn but to accept. Acting this way meant I only ended up hurting myself -- for longer than needed!

Forgiveness frees us from anger and tension, which can have good effects on our health. Accepting, trying to empathise a little and then letting go – forgiveness sets you free.

Freedom is so important, its meaning different to us all. You may not feel free right now, this may feel distant, but it's possible.

During lockdown I found freedom in spending lots of precious moments at home, no longer rushing. I learnt not to give myself a hard time. Since then, I'm able to forgive and let go of the negative stuff, including the people who don't make me feel good; this generates personal freedom.

Knowing I can let go means I'm continuing to work on freeing myself, my mind. Practising mindfulness and meditation have enabled me to do this. If you can just let go of one harmful thought even for a moment, whatever it is for you, you can feel freedom within and then you can build on that.

Forgive yourself for something you've held on to. Free your mind today.

The burden of blame

OFTEN, BY HOLDING on to emotions such as blame and hatred you are the one who ends up hurting the most. The person you're angry with is very unlikely to be sitting at home thinking about how you feel.

By forgiving you can let go of the burden of blame. Such emotions do not help you in any way. Only then can you move forward.

Blaming others is all too easy to do – I've done it many times before. Ultimately, we are responsible for how we feel, so surely it's much better to feel good rather than angry and hateful?

Try and forgive someone or something you've been holding on to … **Forgiveness frees you.**

Close your eyes, take a deep breath, settle.

- Acknowledge the hurt.
- Consider how the pain has affected you.
- Accept that you cannot change the past.
- Determine whether you will forgive.
- Allow yourself time to repair.
- Learn from the situation.
- Forgive and let go.
- Use your energy to focus on what you need: let go of the rest and move forward.

Exhale, release and open your eyes.

***

THERE ARE SO many benefits of forgiveness, it:

- Frees our minds.
- Opens the door for healthier relationships.
- Creates inner strength.
- Paves the path for spiritual happiness.
- Improves mental health and self-esteem.
- Lowers blood pressure and stress levels.
- Reduces symptoms of depression and anxiety.
- Builds a stronger immune system.
- Improves your heart health.
- Calms us.

***

The imperfections are the perfections. – **Anon**

Imperfections are not inadequacies; they are reminders that we're all in this together. – **Brené Brown**

To SEE SOMEONE genuinely happy in their own skin is inspiring beyond words. Living without judgement of themselves, at ease with who they are, 'imperfections and all', is beautiful! When you find your soulmate, you love that imperfect person perfectly.

I recently read 'the word "imperfect" spells "I'm perfect"!' Because everyone is perfect in their own imperfect ways. Embrace your imperfections – they make you uniquely perfect!

Accept yourself.

You are beautiful, you just need to accept who you are. The more you accept yourself the happier you become.

If you spend much of the time worrying if you will fit in or look right or are worthy, you will be forever searching. Only when you love and accept yourself will you really start enjoying all you have as then you will know you deserve it.

Reminder – once more look into the mirror and tell yourself:

I am beautiful.
I am enough.
I open my heart and trust.
I forgive myself.
Now add your own!

Repeat as many times as you like and remember to always notice how you feel.

***

TO HAVE BETTER self-esteem we must search all parts of ourselves, even those parts we find difficult to accept.

Happiness and acceptance go together. Once you accept you are good enough, you're not to blame, you've done all you can, the happiness will start flowing. Whatever you're holding on to – forgive yourself, let it go and accept it's happened. To be beautiful means to be at ease, be comfortable in your own skin, at peace with who you are. That means being at peace with things in the past that have been and things you have no control over changing. When you accept this, happiness really glows.

***

'We don't meet people by accident. They are meant to cross our paths for a reason.' – **Anon**

I LOVE THIS. I too believe that people come into our lives for a reason.

You won't like all the people who come into your life but there is always a reason they come. Some come for a short while, some quickly pass through and others are there for the long haul. The lessons learnt are important for our growth and shape us into who we are.

We learn to love, to forgive, to heal. Learn new skills, see different views, try new things. Perhaps we would rather a certain someone had not come into our lives. Or we keep hold of others a little too long, but there's always a reason, a lesson to be learnt.

We learn from our mistakes and grow wiser. The more wisdom we have the better informed we are to make decisions going forward, creating a wonderful path.

***

BE KIND, TAKE a breath. You grow through what you go through. We are with us all the way.

We can't escape ourselves. We are the one constant who will stick by our side, the one certainty that will be with us to the end so it's kind of handy if we like that person and show that person a little love, don't you think? Even if we have days where we may want to be different or get away from it all. Wherever we get away to, we will still be there in that moment and the next one …

Rather than try and escape, stay and find yourself! Learn to love each part of you on a journey of self-discovery. Once you start on this journey, being present in each moment, without always rushing forward or trying to look back, you can start to find the peace you may have already searched a lifetime for and really enjoy things you never did before. Don't search for happiness in a new car, a new home or some new clothes. Sure, it's nice to have new things but can you feel happiness in all that you love and feel in front of you right now. Can you close your eyes and feel it inside? If you're always striving for the next thing, the next holiday, the next day out, you'll miss all the wonder of today. Enjoy this moment! And this one …

We can't always change what is happening externally, but we can change the way we deal with things. We can find new skills or tools to deal with different situations.

Like Jon Kabat-Zinn says, 'You can't stop the waves, but you can learn to surf!'

Mindfulness enables you to surf those waves that rise in your mind. You can't stop thoughts and situations arising but you sure can learn to manage them.

*⁎⁎

The Journey to Who She Was, Who She's Always Been

Feeling so unworthy, reduced beneath the pain,
My heart it aches so silently, I feel I'm going insane.
Trying to please others, shower them with love,
But all I do is suffocate; nothing ever seems enough.
The habits creep in quietly, the patterns they return,
I feel the call within my soul, there's more that I must learn.
The road looks long, my path it is unknown,
Yet all laid out if I lean in, the call from in my soul.
My strength it speaks up softly, present in the form of tears,
That once I named my weakness for many passing years.
Writing down my feelings, the page it listens more,
To what I have to say inside, to open up new doors.

No longer feeling silenced, my voice begins to grow,
Expressing more of my journey, and what I've come to know.
That pain and much confusion makes sense now in my head,
My heart it whispers louder now, the journey I no longer dread.
Coming home to all I am, living being free,
Finally, I'm not ashamed to be seen, to just be me.
Speaking kindly to myself, compassion replaces words once spoken, words that were simply mean,
The journey to who she was, to who she's always been.

***

Chapter 13

The Journey to Who She Was, Who She's Always Been

And then there was you, looking back at me. Tired eyes, yet a sparkle sat within them. A little older now, too, but the smile still ever-present. The journey to get here tough, a bumpy path trodden. How you got to this point I still don't know but you're here, still showing up and I love you.

I looked in the mirror, and there I was. All grown up, yet in many ways I felt like the teenager I had once been, only wiser, more knowing and finally appreciating all parts of myself. I still don't understand why I've been sent the endless heartbreaking lessons that I have but I'm now grateful for them, and grateful too for each person who has come into my life in some way and what they've taught me.

***

Living your life fully is so important. Being able to get to a point where you truly know who you are, one hundred per cent happy to be you and not constantly trying to fit in with other people's ideals and expectations. I've found this to be one of the hardest parts of reconnecting with myself, but to create space for what's truly meant to be, I see now that letting go is the only way to make room to fully feel and embrace our own weathers and seasons.

Let it all unfold beautifully, with no attachment to time. When you remove the clock, the hands of time, how much freedom do you feel? No more deadlines. Can you ease the need for control? For as long as I can remember I always needed to have a plan, to be in control, unable to let things unfold in their own time. Yet now I see the beauty in a flower: it doesn't try and keep up with the next one, it blooms in its own time. Depending on the conditions this may take a little longer but when the right environment presents, the flower unfolds just as she should. I've always had the tendency to rush. I want things done, then moving to the next. The thing is, the next keeps coming, so when does the rushing stop? It doesn't!

Being in control made me feel safe. Through the difficult, anxious times, being in control gave me something to focus on other than my health. I was always keeping busy – that or being distracted. I simply wouldn't relax and then resented anyone else relaxing! Ironic! How dare they take some time out when I haven't got a moment. The thing is, I see now I had plenty of those moments, I just refused to take them.

Lockdown forced me to slow down. It wasn't easy. It began with intense periods of sheer dread, not being able to continue with my life as busy as I once knew it. Yet each day that passed by, I saw I was getting a little better at easing into things unfolding in their own time. I slowly began to discover who I was beneath the busyness. Slowly my short meditations built up and I detached from the notion of regulation.

I noticed new things and saw that everything still gets done without the stress. Of course, there are still days where I slip into being in control, but I am finding balance ... finally.

Stopping is just as important as getting to the next thing. I appreciate we do need structure and routine, but not all the time. We all end up where we are meant to be, so why not enjoy things coming and going naturally, if we can? Have a bit of time for yourself.

Now that I've learnt to relax, I wake up at the same time, without an alarm. Looking back, the thought of the alarm is what stressed me out before I even went to sleep! The habitual cycle stuck in the mind.

My children are unfolding beautifully with a little less nagging from me. Half the time I now see I wasn't even giving them the time unfold. At times I bubble wrapped them with control and safety.

Things will keep moving forward, changing, growing. We can't control this, so why not let go of the reins, of what we think we 'should' be doing and kick back.

I'm now completely in awe of less is more.

Remember: breathe. Breathe again. It's already happening, so why not notice it?

***

Everything you need is already within

YOU HAVE IT all inside. Trust yourself, trust the process. If you're struggling to see it, notice the struggle, explore it, journal a little. There is no need to force it, just simply notice and then notice once more. Let the answers come to you.

Remember that the only way out is through, and the journey is often easier without force. It's not always quicker, but healing takes time. Be with what is there for you today without trying to change it and allow it to be.

When you stop searching, you arrive here, now and in this moment you discover you are enough as you are – simply that!

***

A GROUNDBREAKING MOMENT for me, was when reading a certain page in *The Boy, The Mole, The Fox and The Horse*. My best discovery is that I am enough as I am! Thirty-nine years later! It took me over a year to read this without welling up, but I kept reading it and let the emotion come. Now I can read it and see that I see that I am enough as I am … and so are you!

Charlie himself told me this at The Cheltenham Literature festival in 2023. I opened my well-used copy of his brilliant book and turned to this very page. He wrote: 'Kelly – You are more than enough. Love, Charlie.'

I am starting to actually believe it a little now, I hope you believe it too.

***

ONE OF THE most helpful things I've accomplished for myself in my lifetime is to find my way back home, to me. I'd run away from myself for so long, buried parts of me I didn't like, hidden behind other versions of me to fit in. All the while this suppression of anxiety built up inside of me until I eventually reached a point where I couldn't get through a single day without experiencing fear.

I've always enjoyed writing, a way of speaking to myself and having time to let out how I feel. But after being suffocated by anxiety for a long time I couldn't even write a sentence about how I felt. I didn't give myself time, I'd lost my ability to open up, lean in and feel it. Now writing has become part of my healing process. I write when I feel down, sad or lost; when I'm confused or overwhelmed. I write when I'm not quite sure what it is I'm feeling or what I want to say, or at times when there is no one to listen. It turns out I seem to have a lot to say and in turn a lot to write: endless notes and long messages spilling over! What I do know is that the simple act of writing my thoughts and feelings down has been a huge part of the journey to where I am today.

Looking through some of the notes and stories I have written I now see how lost I was, how afraid. How the suppressed emotion was desperate to spill out in some way. Hidden behind fear, chocolate, keeping busy – the list goes on. Reading and listening to other books I know I am not alone in feeling this way; none of us are. Sometimes we must reach the toughest points in our lives just before something amazing happens, leading us to find out who we are.

To sit still and be comfortable with this is a joy. A racing mind and feeling overwhelmed is anything but a joy. People may judge this book, have a different opinion to what I have written but after spending so much time hiding behind excuses and fears I decided to share this, what I discovered, what has helped me. All along, much of what led me astray was that desperation to be loved, to fit in.

So, this was my aim, through this very book: my journey back to me, without delving into each trauma, instead sharing a summary of what I have so far discovered, that which has helped me. I hope it provides you with something you can use to move forward and enable you to see just how amazing your life is. To see just how wonderful you already are.

```
Sitting in silence, the sun burning down on
my skin, I knew I'd arrived. I had accepted
me, I had compassion towards myself.
```

***

MY WORLD HAS felt tough. Just when I thought it was settling, with real love enveloping me, I would be rudely jolted back to this heavy feeling in my heart. It weighed me down, I never thought I'd get back up, but somehow, I did.

Tedious, relentless, angry, not good enough, too emotional, too much. I heard this again and again – hearing it from other people and telling myself – and I believed it for a while, a few decades. I'd try and fit in once more and people around me seemed happier, but inside, I was losing me. Fearful to be honest, to be me. I didn't want to be rejected again. What was the alternative?

I'd always put my time in someone else's hands, my feelings too, passing blame and not accepting what I had to face, not brave enough. I found it easier to shrink instead of standing up and be me. That niggle would keep rising again to make changes, but so often I would just wait.

For a long time, I was afraid to feel nothing. I would rather feel bad than feel nothing at all, thinking this made me feel more alive. The truth of the matter was I was burning out. Now free from this way of thinking it's so clear to me now the unhelpful habits I clung on to.

Knowing that I can look after myself and I need not fear all the things that had been standing in my way.

We can never escape ourselves: to be free we must find ourselves and the only way to do this is to connect within.

No matter where you go, there you always are. – **Jon Kabat-Zinn**

We are always with ourselves and the sooner we see who we are, we back ourselves and know we are there for us, the sooner we are happier in our own company.

***

Thankfulness

THE SIMPLE ACT of being thankful creates a change within yourself. Practising thankfulness and being grateful, writing and sharing thoughts, getting them out of my head onto paper has made me realise so much.

So, a big thank you to every one of you reading this and taking some time for you. I started writing to help heal myself, I never knew it would blossom the way it has. One page led to another – one page at a time, my thoughts, feelings and experiences followed. I can express how I honestly feel and share how mindfulness and meditation – along with breathing techniques, journaling, gratitude and so much more –have helped me overcome this. By sharing the things that I've found helped me, I hope they help you too.

I simply kept coming back to what I heard in my heart and that message was to share this part of my journey beyond my journals and Instagram page. I used to reserve sharing my writing for fear of what I said being judged, not being good enough or simply being taken from me, but along the way the clarity in individuality shines above it all. I am truly grateful for the quotes I come across which evoke questions inside my soul; the conversations shared to explore something deeper; the ears that have opened to let my own words land, inspire discussion and in turn shape my healing, developing my own style when I teach; the music that has held me, throughout life, carried me through the darkest times, holding that safe space for me to cry, to remember, to love. This all part of the journey: back to this very moment.

***

THERE IS ALWAYS something to be thankful for, so many things in fact.

If you only say one prayer in a day, make it thank you. – **Rumi**

This is one of the quotes I kept coming back to when struggling, and I still do it now. I can't begin to tell you about the change within me through this little step. We often find it easy to be down on ourselves, but talking to ourselves in this way feeds this narrative and takes us away from what matters. Hard times come for us all but in being simply grateful the story can begin to change.

Even through recent heartache, I'm so thankful for the wonderful times I have had, I'll never forget these.

You're free to enjoy you

No two paths are the same, but many may lead to the same destination. It doesn't mean your path is going the wrong way, simply the path you were meant to take to arrive here today unfolds in your own time and in your own way. Your path may take longer to reach the destination, but that's ok, you are where you are and that's exactly where you're meant to be. Everyone has their own journey, their own views. Let things unfold in their own time.

If you feel overwhelmed, take it step by step, be with what is here for you today. Do what you are ready for, make changes that feel right for you and live your life with broad brush strokes, but know that it's ok to put the brush down at times too.

Find your way back to you.

***

Truth

The truth is hard to come by, but mostly with yourself,
In time if you don't face it, it impacts on your health.
Burying your story, it pushed down deep inside,
The person stood before you, lost through other people's eyes.
To speak it leaves you lonely, no space to freely share,
The attack quiet in your body, yet the strength holds like a bear.
You try to say your feelings, emotions running wild,
Yet held back from your freedom, the voice of inner child.
Nobody to listen, your voice falls on deaf ears,
So again, the truth pushed down, passing by the years.
You silence the connection, too deep within yourself.
A lid goes on the jar once more, your truth back on the shelf.
Time is passing quickly, conditioning comes forth,
Yet still you feel the bravery in every path you walk.
Stop. Take time to listen. Reach up to the shelf,
Slowly take your time with it, make space for your health.
There's always time for healing, to open to your soul,
For when you do and speak your truth you begin to see the gold.

You know what's inside of you, you know how it feels,
Let it out and speak your truth, create the space to heal.
Yes, it will be painful, people slip away,
But what's meant for you won't pass you by and those who matter, stay.
At times it will feel lonely, the sadness feels too much,
But sharing who you truly are, you don't know whose lives you'll touch.
Keep the ripple going, don't hide who you are,
The energy and openness, a galaxy of stars.
In quiet and reflection, the bravery it blooms,
Strength to be here as you are and show up in the room.
Look how far you've come now, be grateful for your youth.
The time has come for you now to move forward with your truth.

**When we build habits from fear, we lose ourselves.
When we build habits from love, we find ourselves.**

Kelly Saward

Mindful Moments

IN THIS SECTION I share quick, accessible tips for whenever you need to take a mindful moment. A moment is all it takes … remember, be kind to yourself.

I WANT TO start this Mindful Moments section with this well-known 'wheel of emotions', devised by psychologist Robert Plutchik. You can see that emotions are numerous and complex, and we all feel each of these at some point in the day, week, or month. However, we often lack the vocabulary to communicate exactly how we feel in any given moment.

The next time you are journaling or you've finished a meditation and you know you feel *something*, but you're not sure exactly what it is, take a look at this wheel of emotion. See if it can help you identify what that emotion is that you're feeling. First noticing what you feel, then exploring why you feel that way, remembering there is no right or wrong answer.

The more in tune you can become with your emotions, and the feelings that spark them, the easier it becomes to identify what you need in that moment.

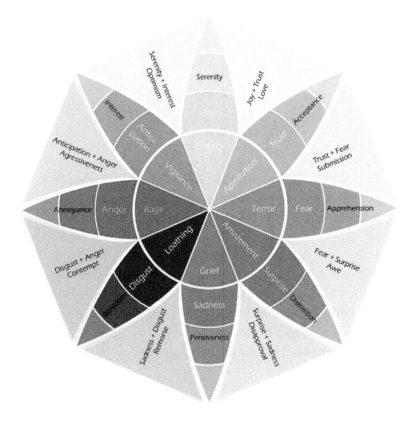

Figure 1. Plutchik's wheel of emotions (image credit: Pinterest)

Everyone you know is fighting a battle you know nothing about. Be kind. Always – **Robin Williams**

When finding yourself remember this: on the outside things may appear fine but quite often everybody is struggling with something they'd rather not bring to the surface. The media, Facebook, Instagram, TikTok, YouTube – there are endless streams where we can see how others are living their lives. People making judgements all the time. Celebrities quite often full of smiles and a seamless face. Yet under it all there may be pain, hurt, sadness; just as there is with any one of us.

Globally we do need to be kinder. Always. This message doesn't change. Battles are being faced every day, and a simple act of kindness or support could give that person the strength they need to ask for help. But be kind to yourself, too.

It may not feel like it at times, but in every open space – those spaces you now give yourself permission to access – you are releasing all the time, finding your way back to you, to freedom, to a point where joy is found in having lunch by yourself and that is simply enough. These spaces are no longer denied.

Be kind to your mind

It COULD NOT be more important to be kind to your mind, to yourself. When you realise the importance of this, the rest will naturally follow. It is not selfish or a waste of time. (As I told myself many times in the past.)

We are happy to do good for others, check in and make sure friends and family are ok. Tell others to take a break and slow down. But do you ever apply this to yourself? Do you ever explore the emotions you are feeling and why?

We know the benefits of eating healthily and how exercise is good for us – there are resources available on this everywhere you look. But the mind often sits in unknown territory, not top priority and unless you look a little deeper, the vast amount of health benefits accessible stays unknown. We are lucky that as time goes on there is more focus on feeling, emotional wellbeing and mental health but because much of this can't be seen on the surface, it still doesn't take precedence and often remains on the back foot.

Mental health isn't something to be ashamed of, it isn't something to hide. Just as if you had broken a bone you'd require rest and recuperation, the same care should be applied to those illnesses we can't see. We navigate through life the best we can, sometimes questions hanging, the mind bruised from steps we take and what we live through, and over time if we don't acknowledge and feel it, the healing slips further away.

If we only focus on healthy habits for our body, then we will end up leaving the mind behind, and the body will suffer anyway.

Mind caring tips

- Stop. Don't spend all day rushing.
- Get outside for a while.
- Feel the sun on your face (if it's out!).
- Feel the rain on your skin (if it's raining!).
- Connect with nature.
- Notice your breathing today.
- Meditate – just a few minutes of noticing where you are presently.

- Write in a journal.
- Notice what you do have.
- List some things you are grateful for (as many as you like).
- Stretch, dance, walk – feel your movements.
- Listen to some music.
- Laugh – watch something funny.
- Freely sit with how you feel without judgement.
- Draw, doodle, colour.
- Word searches, sudokus, crosswords.

Above all, be available to look after your mind. Look after it and in turn it looks after you.

**

5-4-3-2-1

A USEFUL TECHNIQUE I use again and again when I want to get out of my head and into my body is the 5-4-3-2-1 method.

It's a great grounding technique, especially in the height of panic, anxiety or overwhelm – it's easy for children to follow, too. Not only does it tune into each of the senses, but you notice more, you experience more and if you have ever experienced a panic attack or anxiety, then this is worth remembering.

Sight, touch, sound, smell, taste
Focus on 5 things you can SEE.

Find 4 things you can FEEL.
Name 3 things that you can HEAR.
Notice 2 things you can SMELL.
Lastly, 1 thing you can TASTE.

You can do this as many times as you need, until you feel grounded. You can also use this when you're not feeling anxious or stressed. It can be used as a pleasurable exercise to bring you into the present moment, creating awareness of what you see, touch, hear, smell and taste.

Give it a try now or just come back to it if you need.

Audio link for 5-4-3-2-1 meditation:
https://www.room478.com/54321/

Walking in nature

AN EFFECTIVE WAY to help reduce stress, anxiety and depression – and maybe even improve your memory – is to take a walk in the woods; surround yourself in nature.

Research in a growing scientific field called ecotherapy has shown a strong connection between time spent in nature and reduced stress, anxiety and depression.

Anxiety is a natural human response when we perceive that we are under threat, which activates the fight-or-flight response. Calming nature sounds and even outdoor silence can lower blood pressure and levels of the stress hormone cortisol, calming the body's fight-or-flight response. Just a twenty- to thirty-minute walk in nature can reverse this stress response, keeping you in a more relaxed state of mind.

Try taking a mindful walk today.

Box breathing

THIS IS SUCH a great way to take a moment and notice your breath. You'll feel the benefit just by taking a moment or two. Practising this can help you regulate your breath, too.

Look at any square or rectangular shape in the space you are in. You could even use your phone or this book.

- Start by bringing your attention to the top left-hand corner and breathe in as you let your attention follow the line to the top right-hand corner.
- Hold your breath here for a second, and let your attention run down the right-hand side, still holding your breath until you reach the bottom right-hand corner.
- At this point begin exhaling, letting your attention

run from the bottom right-hand corner to the bottom left-hand corner as you breathe out.

- Then hold your breath again at this point as your attention flows from the bottom left-hand corner back to the starting point at the top left-hand corner.

You can repeat this as many times as you like.

Audio link for box breathing meditation: https://www.room478.com/box-breathing/

Hand breathing

YOUR HANDS ARE **always accessible, so whenever you need to connect with your breathing they are a great tool to use to gain focus and use as a prompt.**

- Hold out your hands in front of you, notice them, bringing awareness to how they feel, such as the temperature of your hands.
- Then choose a hand to start with and bring your

forefinger to the outside edge of the opposite thumb, with your finger at the part where your thumb meets your hand.

- As you bring attention to your next inhale allow your finger to run up your thumb. Then as you exhale, run your finger down the inside of your thumb.
- Repeat this motion as you draw around each finger, breathing in as you move up and breathing out as you go back down.
- When you finish that hand, notice how it feels compared to your other hand.
- Repeat on the opposite side.
- Notice how both your hands now feel.

When looking at your hands, remember to notice your breath. Where do you feel it in your body?

Audio link for hand breathing meditation:
https://www.room478.com/hand-breathing/

Letting go meditation – balloon

IT CAN BE difficult to let go, but it is possible. Often by looking at how we hold on, in turn we learn how to loosen our grip ever so slowly and eventually we are free. Try this short meditation to practise letting go of any unwanted thoughts you have today.

Close your eyes if this feels comfortable.

Just begin to notice your breath in its natural rhythm, not trying to change it in any way.

Allow yourself to connect with who you are, in this moment. Any feelings of anxiety that arise, just allow them to be present and on your next exhale give them a little space.

Bring in compassion, care, kindness, acceptance; whatever you need.

Ask yourself, what do you need? Where do you feel this need in your body?

Just allow yourself to settle, once again, awareness of your body – your breath.

As you notice your breath in your body, notice how it comes and goes. As you sit, do just this: simply notice which thoughts drift into your mind and then leave again, no longer present. That ebb and flow, the coming and going. Just observing.

On your next inhale we are going to explore letting go of

thoughts that arise.

If you feel comfortable, I want you to close your eyes if you haven't already and picture yourself standing somewhere peaceful, somewhere comforting to you. If it feels ok for you, try to picture yourself outside. Wherever feels right for you.

When you have visualised this place I want you to picture yourself standing, aware of your body and bring your attention to your breath.

Just see where this feels most comfortable for you, allowing your breath to fill your body, breathing in your natural rhythm and just be aware of any thoughts that may arise.

Aware of your breath once more, I want you to picture in your mind a tree. Think of this tree with strong roots, a solid trunk.

The day is warm, the sun is shining and you lean up against this tree.

Breathing in you connect with the tree, you feel its strength. Above you the branches and leaves are blowing in the wind. It feels unsettling up there but you breathe in again and feel the strength of the tree behind you, the solid roots under your feet.

We often have thoughts that arise in our minds – some helpful, some not.

As a thought arises I want you to picture this thought leaving out the top of your head and disappearing above into the wind through the blowing branches.

You can label the thoughts if you like, and see them leave through the top of your head and disappear out of sight.

You breathe in, still strong against the trunk of the tree.

Bring yourself back to your breath and if another thought enters your mind just do the same again. If you find the thoughts sticking, reach out your hand. In front of you there are some balloons, a whole bunch of them. Take one, notice the colour of it, feel the ribbon in your hand and place your thought inside the balloon. Then when you're ready just let go of the ribbon in your hand and watch it float away.

If you notice your mind clinging on to your thoughts or trying to push them away just observe this impulse to do so.

Our thoughts and fears are not who we are, with practice we learn to let these go.

If you can't let go, just try the opposite – really hold on and see how that feels for you. By looking at how you hold on to your thoughts, you will then learn to let go.

Now, just be aware of your breath and how just like our thoughts it comes and goes. Each breath filling your body with comfort, a deeper sense of grounding yourself. Coming to your next breath and being aware of your posture, just take a deep breath and stretch. As you exhale gently open your eyes.

Allow yourself a moment to reflect on your experience and journal on this if you want to.

Audio link for balloon meditation:
https://www.room478.com/letting-go-meditation/

Affirmations

THE WAY WE talk to ourselves matters. Spend a moment or two saying some affirmations to yourself or write them down. You can use the prompts throughout the book or make up your own. Here are a few to get you started.

I trust myself.
I am confident.
I am exactly where I'm meant to be.

Remember this is your story, your experience, your journey. Choose things that fit with you, that feel right.

Journal

I HAVE MENTIONED it throughout my story, this book. Journal when you can! Write notes, poems, words … simply write it out.

If you are feeling stuck with where to start, trying using a prompt. Make your own prompts or flick back through this book (or any other book that you like) and see what you are drawn to, what you want to explore more, ask your own questions.

Prompts …

What do you need?
How do you feel?
Which emotions aren't you yet ready to feel?
What pain sits so deep?
What's your go-to addictive behaviour when you don't want to face something?

Feel it all. Exploration by poetry …

Ask yourself a question, allow it time to be,
Not forced yet just unfolding, present naturally.

Feel into your body, let it rise again,
Notice what is present then let it all descend.

Allow some time to wonder, simply to explore,
No need to even rush it or reach again for more.

This story yours to walk through, there is no right or wrong.
Occasionally just let yourself listen to your song.

Your voice it has the answers, discovery inside.
The doubt yes it arises, but the space to see is wide.

Beyond the not believing, below the voice of doubt.
Just breathe into your body and let your truth come out.

Keep exploring, questioning and allow yourself to feel whatever it is. In turn the healing follows, and the freedom in sight.

Audio link for Journal:
https://www.room478.com/journal/

Chakras – our energy centres

BELOW I HAVE listed the most common energy centres that are referred to. However, there is further understanding available should you wish to delve deeper. *Becoming Supernatural: How Common People Are Doing the Uncommon* by Dr Joe Dispenza is a great place to start for further reading.

Root – Our foundation, the place we withstand challenge, find steadiness. Element: Earth. Colour: Red. Crystal: Hematite.

Sacral – A place of abundance, sexual connection, creativity. Element: Water. Colour: Orange. Crystal: Tigers Eye.

Solar Plexus – Self-acceptance, confidence, self-worth, a place of control. Element: Fire. Colour: Yellow. Crystal: Amber.

Heart – The place we give and receive love; access openness, compassion. Element: Air. Colour: Green. Crystal: Rose Quartz.

Throat – The place of communication, our voice, what do you have to say? Element: Sound. Colour: Light Blue. Crystal: Aquamarine.

Third Eye – Seeing the bigger picture, the eyes of the soul, where we explore what can't be seen. Element: Light. Colour: Purple. Crystal: Amethyst.

Crown – Fully connected, light and love. Element: Divine Consciousness. Colour: White/Violet. Crystal: Clear Quartz.

If you want to, you can explore the following meditation for clearing through the energy centres.

Chakra clearing meditation

Remove blocks, notice resistance.

Use this guided meditation to allow the energy flow in your body to simply be observed and move through, bringing a gentle, easier flow of energy to move through your energy centres.

Closing down your eyes, become aware of your breathing. Just notice the inhale as it enters your body; the subtle pause in between we often miss and the flow of energy as you exhale again.

Repeat this, simply noticing your breath. Thoughts will come; just notice them too and bring your attention back to your body as and when you notice.

Breathing in
Breathing out.
Breathing in; notice the pause.
Breathing out; notice the pause.

Picture yourself stood up against the trunk of a tree, possibly a familiar one, or one you feel connected to.

Feel your body supported by the tree, the comfort as you close your eyes if you haven't already.

Your breath coming and going; you are simply just noticing that as and when you remember.

Now bring your attention to the soles of your feet, their connection with the ground, the earth beneath them. As you breathe in, draw energy from the ground and feel this coming into the soles of your feet. Notice if a colour is present with this energy and simply note this in your mind.

As you exhale the grounding energy moving through, with every inhale, with every breath you draw more energy in. This filtering from the soles of your feet, over your toes, throughout both feet, gently moving through your ankles, into your lower legs, up over your knees and into your thighs, that energy moving at its own pace.

Notice how you feel. Is there still a colour present? Has it changed?

Explore this for a moment.

Allow your attention to now move up to your root, the base of your spine. Your root – your foundation, the place we withstand challenge, find steadiness. Once more connected with the element of earth. Allow your breath to come and go and as you breathe in see how you feel about breathing in the colour red, associated with this chakra. Simply notice as you breathe in and out … notice, is there any resistance? Or a steady flow of energy? Just simply allow your attention to be here for a moment, letting the energy move through this energy centre, the root. Affirm 'I am clearing the blocks in my body'.

Again, explore changing of colours, easy flow of energy or blocks present and allow your attention to allow this energy to move up into your sacral chakra – a place of abundance, sexual connection, creativity, connecting to the element of water. Allow your breath to come and go and as you breathe in see how you feel about breathing in the colour orange, associated with this chakra. Simply notice as you breathe in and out … notice, is there any resistance? Or a steady flow of energy? Just simply allow your attention to be here for a moment, letting the energy move through this energy centre, the sacral. Affirm, 'I feel the energy in my body'.

Again, explore changing of colours, easy flow of energy or blocks present and allow your attention to allow this energy to move up into your solar plexus, the place of self-acceptance, confidence, self-worth, the place of control connecting to that element fire. Allow your breath to come and go and as you breathe in see how you feel about breathing in the colour yellow, associated with this chakra. Simply notice as you breathe in and out … notice, is there any resistance? Or a steady flow of energy? Just simply allow your attention to be here for a moment, letting the energy move through this energy centre, the solar plexus. Affirm, 'I can observe what is present for me in my body'.

Again, explore changing of colours, easy flow of energy or blocks present and allow your attention to allow this energy to move up into your heart – the place we give and receive love. The place we access openness, compassion, connecting with the element of air. Allow your breath to come and go and as you breathe in see how you feel about breathing in the colour green, associated with this chakra.

Simply notice as you breathe in and out … notice, is there any resistance? Or a steady flow of energy? Just simply allow your attention to be here for a moment, letting the energy move through this energy centre, the heart. Affirm, 'I love myself and my body'.

Again, explore changing of colours, easy flow of energy or blocks present and allow your attention to allow this energy to move up into your throat, the place of communication, your voice: what do you have to say? Connecting with the element of sound. Allow your breath to come and go and as you breathe in see how you feel about breathing in the colour blue, a soft blue present in your throat. Simply notice as you breathe in and out … notice, is there any resistance? Or a steady flow of energy? Just simply allow your attention to be here for a moment, letting the energy move through this energy centre, the throat chakra. Affirm, 'I speak kindly to myself and listen to what I have to say'.

Again, explore changing of colours, easy flow of energy or blocks present and allow your attention to allow this energy to move up in to your third eye – seeing the bigger picture, the eyes of the soul, where we explore what can't be seen. Connecting to the light. Allow your breath to come and go and as you breathe in see how you feel about breathing in the colour purple which is associated with this chakra. Simply notice as you breathe in and out … notice, is there any resistance? Or a steady flow of energy? Just simply allow your attention to be here for a moment, letting the energy move through this energy centre connecting to your third eye, located between your eyebrows. Affirm, 'I am open to what I see, what I seek'.

'What you seek is seeking you' – **Rumi**

Again, explore changing of colours, easy flow of energy or blocks present and allow your attention to allow this energy to move up into your crown chakra, located at the top of your head, this place where you access that point of being fully connected to light and love. Connecting with the divine consciousness. Allow your breath to come and go and as you breathe in see how you feel about breathing in a white or violet light, associated with the crown chakra. Simply notice as you breathe in and out … notice, is there any resistance? Or a steady flow of energy? Just simply allow your attention to be here for a moment, letting the energy move through this energy centre, the crown. Affirm 'I know who I am and trust I walk the path meant for me'.

Now bring your attention to the top of your head, picture a little door in the top of your head opening and as the door opens release anything that feels freed up to leave; notice the blocks and allow the flow of energy; allow this clearing to take place, connecting to the universal energy above; finding balance between this and the earth to bring balance into your body as it feels comfortable.

Notice if a colour is present with the motion of the energy, let this cleanse your body, a flow coming in through the crown of your head and allow it to softly pour into your body and move back though your body, each muscle relaxing as it flows through.

Bring your attention back to your feet and release once more out of the soles of your feet, clearing anything left behind back to the earth, and as you do allow the little door at the top of your head to close.

Feeling your back against the tree and gaining strength from this, your body strong and any thoughts that arise, just allow them to leave your mind and float off through the branches overhead.

Breathing in
Breathing out.

Breathing in; notice the pause.
Breathing out; notice the pause.

Breathing in
Breathing out.

Breathing in; notice the pause.
Breathing out; notice the pause.

Now expand your attention from inside your body to this moment, feeling the ground beneath, becoming aware of where you are sitting right now. Notice any sounds you can hear in this present moment. Checking in with your body's temperature, tune into how you feel.

Taking a nice deep breath in, feeling the clear flow of energy in your body.

Breathing out and gently opening your eyes.

Take a moment to reflect on your experience.

Audio link for chakra clearing meditation:
https://www.room478.com/chakra-balance/

Energy clearing

My PERSONAL TIPS for clearing your energy, the ones I enjoy the most:

- Have a shower and visualise the clearing through your body, like sand washing away from every part of your skin.
- Use palo santo or sage for smudging and allow this smoke to clear for you.
- Use sound or instruments. I have a lovely rain stick and crystal bowls, but you can use sound of any form.
- Go into the forest, put your bare feet on the ground, feel the earth. Nature is cleansing.
- Get to the sea, put your feet in, your body in, and feel the clearing take place.
- Use incense, diffusers, crystals and salts.
- Meditation (either guided or in silence) and sound

waves: different frequencies will help depending on where you're at.

There are so many ways to clear energy. The most important thing is to always remember to find what works for you.

***

I AM ALWAYS learning more about how to incorporate a mindful moment into your day, so please stay connected with me via YouTube and Instagram for my latest updates and thoughts.

YouTube – @Room478 and @fiveminutethoughts
Instagram – @room_478

Free audible versions of all exercises and meditations throughout the book.

Recommended Reading List

Brené Brown – *Atlas of the Heart: Mapping Meaningful Connection and the Language of Human Experience* (2021)

Rebecca Campbell – *Light is the New Black: A Guide to Answering Your Soul's Callings and Working Your Light* (2015)

Dr Joe Dispenza – *Becoming Supernatural: How Common People are Doing the Uncommon* (2017)

Kirsty Gallagher – *Lunar Living: Working with the Magic of the Moon Cycles* (2020)

Héctor García – *Ikigai: The Japanese Secret to a Long and Happy Life* (2017)

Dawn Huebner – *What to do When You Worry Too Much: A Kid's Guide to Overcoming Anxiety* (2005)

Jon Kabat-Zinn – *Full Catastrophe Living (Revised Edition): How to Cope with Stress, Pain and Illness Using Mindfulness Meditation* (2013)

Charlie Mackesey – *The Boy, The Mole, The Fox and The Horse* (2019)

Mark Manson – *The Subtle Art of Not Giving a F*ck: A Counterintuitive Approach to Living a Good Life* (2016)

Matthew McConaughey – *Greenlights* (2020)

Elizabeth Gilbert – *Eat Pray Love: One Woman's Search for Everything* (2009)

Elizabeth Gilbert – *Big Magic: How to Live a Creative Life, and Let Go of Your Fear* (2016)

Mark Williams & Danny Penman – *Mindfulness: A Practical Guide to Finding Peace in a Frantic World* (2011)

Eline Snel – *Sitting Still Like a Frog: Mindfulness Exercises for Kids (and Their Parents)* (2013)

Jay Shetty – *Think Like A Monk: The Secret of how to Harness the Power of Positivity and be Happy Now* (2020)

Michael A. Singer – *The Untethered Soul: The Journey Beyond Yourself* (2007)

Ekhart Tolle – *The Power of Now: A Guide to Spiritual Enlightenment* (1997)

Ekhart Tolle – *Milton's Secret: An Adventure of Discovery Through Then, When, and the Power of Now* (2008)

Acknowledgements

When I first used writing to explore my thoughts, I simply enjoyed jotting down whatever came to me. Then there came a point when I realised I had overcome a sense of shame or judgement about what I'd written and I wanted to share my little notes of self-discovery with you. On reflection, this book naturally unfolded. And now here it is: a part of my healing laid out in front of me and now here in front of you in the hope it helps you as well.

I couldn't have brought this book to life without the love and support I had surrounding me, which at times I didn't notice. From the bottom of my heart, I hold thanks to so many for being by my side in some way during this process, in my life. Thank you to everyone on my journey but there are a few people in the past year who have really given me the love and support I needed during my writing process, checking in and lifting me up. The little things have always been the big things to me and the way to my heart. Thank you for you.

To my amazing daughters, Olivia and Summer, for believing in me and despite the windy road of having me as a mum, I always feel the unconditional love, the joy and inspiring moments in every single day. You are both such a credit to me.

To Olivia, for being my final proofreader, for giving me your time and advice, you inspire me every day and just blow me away. Thank you for giving me an ear unconditionally and being there always, I am so grateful, and learn endlessly from you: you are so wonderful.

To Summer for having the strength to shine above any difficulties, to express your words so beautifully and free yourself. Your words of wisdom straight into my heart, you feel what I feel and in turn help me move through too, you are so amazing.

To Mark, despite many bumps in the road, thank you for loving me, for never trying to change me, for letting me be free to always follow my heart, whatever that looks like, for leaving the cage door open.

To James, my amazing little brother who is simply my rock and even writing this the emotion and love is huge and the trust I have for you. I am so grateful for your support, and the tremendous laughs like I simply don't get with anyone else in the same way. Thank you for you and not forgetting your amazing wife – my sister-in-law, Vicky – the sister I never had, who is just a wonderful, loving and supportive person. Thank you both for listening to me, reading this book, and giving me advice along the way.

To Mum and Dad. The parents I chose to bring me the lessons and love I have received and brought me to this point today. I love you both so much and I wouldn't change any of my life and all its experiences, without which I wouldn't be *where* I am today or *be* the person I am today – that person

I now love with all my heart as much as I love both of you.

To Siân, well what can I say! I believe things happen for a reason and when I had the strength to cling on to that belief inside me, that inner knowing I wanted to share my writing for real this time, you popped up on my feed and I reached out. From the moment we spoke I knew I wanted you to help me, and you've helped me more than I thought possible! Thank you for being a wonderful editor and really guiding me though this unknown process to bring my book to life, for being real and sharing you with me too … beyond thankful for you. Thank you for being patient with my stream of questions and mostly for reminding me, I can do this! Thank you for holding my hand from afar. Thank you also for the recommendations for the final pieces to bring the vision of my book to life.

Theo Johnson, who helped me bring my vision of this book cover alive, which meant a lot as to me it tells my story. Thank you for your patience, which you needed a lot of with me, whilst we went back and forth a fair few times, you've been amazing. I am very grateful.

Becky Warrak, who came along towards the end to help me in those final stages of layout and getting the book live, which again I needed. Your friendly, knowledgeable manner enabled me to see it's happening!

To Stacey, you have been there all the way through; my oldest friend. Through the madness and the tears, being at my door after the breakdown despite me saying I was ok. You've always welcomed my emotion – however much I needed to release – with open arms, and in turn shared all of yours with me. I can never thank you enough for you. Seeing your tears when I told you about this book, then feeling the love and belief from you has meant the world, even you listening to me lately as I relate everything we feel to the moon! I need to say this: you are loved.

To Laura, my soul sister and my fellow witch – I'm so proud to say that! I feel I've known you forever and you have helped me believe, listened to me, guided me and quite frankly you are my personal earth angel! Whenever that doubt surfaced you shut it down. We went into the vortex and blimey, it's great up there. Look at us. Thank you for you.

To Ash for reading my book, listening to my fears and freak-outs and seeing beyond the surface, into my soul, thank you.

To Tone, for really being a support on my journey, more than you will ever know, for listening, checking in and guiding me along the way.

To everyone else I've met and has shaped part of my life outside of this writing journey, I thank you too.

I always wanted to do this properly and for all of you I am so thankful. For every book and quote I've read, every person who's shared their time with me and conversation.

To the authors who do not know me but have inspired me and touched my heart when times felt lonely: Elizabeth Gilbert, Brené Brown and Rebecca Campbell. Not forgetting Kirsty Gallagher.

Last but not least, to my reader, to you, for buying this book and connecting with me, for listening to what I have to say. In turn, I hope you find the freedom to share little parts of you too, to find the freedom in the discoveries of what too may have been hidden for you for so long with no shame or judgement attached and in turn find the love and connection we all seek.

There is nothing more than this.

Final thought ...

FOR ME, PERHAPS the biggest learning of all is seeing the understanding, strength and love present in my daughters. They repeat things back to me I have said, just when I need it, paint beautiful pictures of quotes I have shared and are both wonderful writers. I was so grateful to my eldest daughter for proofreading this very book. Her own writing is exceptional and her aspirations to be an editor herself are inspiring. Writing seems to be present in all of us and at Christmas, my youngest daughter wrote me a poem. With her permission I share this with you.

I wrote you this because I want to express
How much you mean to me even when life is a mess,
I know perfect worlds simply aren't real,
But knowing you're there makes that not a big deal,

I was pondering for hours how even to start,
There are so many things I hold deep in my heart,
Your smile brings me warmth, it lights up my days,
You also have talents in all different ways,

Your eyes, your hair and all of your looks,
You're strong, patient and can even write books,
All of that is good and it's kind,
But what I love most is the girl deep inside,

Sometimes she cries, feels she's not good enough,
But really those things happen to all of us,
Sometimes emotions get too much and spill over,
Though that's how she's tough, and that's why I
love her.

Whilst I was writing I wanted it to be perfect,
I was scribbling down notes, making sure it was
worth it,
I kept deleting lines and I wasn't sure what to do,
So I closed my eyes and I tried picturing you,

I smiled to myself as I took in what I saw,
There was a confident woman I was stood before,
Her hair strung with kindness, her heart soft
and pure,
Her eyes glazed with passion, the ones I adore,

I see her face in the morning sun,
That face is the one that I call my mum,
You make me so proud, so that's why I made this
for you,
I hope you have a great Christmas and a fun one
too.

Summer – Age 11
Christmas 2023.

Work with Me

Kelly Saward
Coach & Speaker

If you felt connected with my book and want to work with me there are many ways to do this.

I am passionate about the work I do. My desire is to share my experience alongside the wonderful things I have learnt and continue to learn. That's why I have written this book and created my workshop too. I want to guide you towards the many doors available to you; free from fear, full of confidence, connected to love.

Available for private and corporate events, festivals, conferences, and anything in-between. If you're looking for a speaker or facilitator at your event, please get touch.

Retreats and Workshops - Mindfulness & Meditation
Group Meditation - 1-2-1 Coaching
Confidence Building - Communication Skills
Emotional Resilience - Anxiety Relief
Workplace Wellbeing - Radio Presenter

If you're struggling with anxiety, lacking in confidence or simply want to connect more deeply to yourself why not book in a 1:1 call to see how I can help you.

'New Doors'
Lead With Love

a personalised workshop for self-discovery; strengthen yourself and your business like never before.

Seasonal programme available
Workshops - Retreats - Team Building - Away days
Connect and nourish - Journal with me

The doors are waiting to be opened, with love ...

Collaborations welcome

come in, create space, free your mind

Contact Details

Kelly Saward

Founder of Room 478
Mindfulness & Meditation
Coach and Speaker

Website: www.room478.com/ .co.uk
Email: hello@room478.co.uk
Instagram: @room_478
YouTube: @Room478 / @fiveminutethoughts

Printed in Great Britain
by Amazon

37748161R00199